Homes
in the
Oregon Forest

Settling Columbia County, 1870-1920

I gratefully inscribe this book to the memory of those early settlers who rest in the various cemeteries, marked or lost to memory, in Columbia county.

Library of Congress Catalog Card Number: 83-71069
ISBN 0-934784-37-X

Printed in the United States of America

Foreword

If a man is fortunate he will, before he dies,
gather up as much as he can of his civilized heritage . . .
and to his final breath he will be grateful for
this inexhaustible legacy . . .

Will Durant

I was born in 1902 in a farmhouse where Tedford creek joins Milton creek, a mile from the adjoining farms of the Tarbells, my maternal grandparents and great-grandparents. Between our places stood the little Yankton schoolhouse, already fifteen years old but with tree stumps and brush still in the unfenced school yard.

My great aunt, Alice Tarbell Brown, wrote that there were no "foreigners" along Milton creek in 1891; most of the people came from Maine. The area was first known as Yankeetown, then as Maineville, as the overwhelming preponderance of early settlers came from Aroostook county, Maine, noted for its lumbering and potatoes.

Not untypically, my mother's family experienced the cycle of home-uprooting and resettlement—not that of the earliest explorers, adventurers, traders and trappers, even not the first wave of venturesome overland ox-cart pioneers. These people came as farmers, settlers, builders, developers— seeking homes back from the main rivers up along the tributaries of the tributaries. They came west on the railroad leaving behind security and settled community life for the unknown future in Oregon's own Northwest corner.

Rich farm land waiting to have timber taken off, and promises of a milder climate beckoned. The early settlers were sometimes disheartened, even disillusioned by the rain and mud; still, many lasted it out and agreed with Lawrence Tarbell, who wrote after twenty years of Milton creek weather, "We have not got rich yet but we do like the state we live in very much."

President Theodore Roosevelt's speech in Chicago in 1899 emphasized, "I wish to preach, not the doctrine of ignoble ease, but the doctrine of the strenuous life." The generation of inner Columbia county settlers from 1870 to 1920 knew well the Roughrider's doctrine. They daily confronted the crude facts of human experience. Here in naked shape was the situation where a little difference in the weather or in the marketplace would mean the difference between an empty or a full belly.

It took a man more than three days' wages to pay for a pair of boots, and a day's work to buy a pair of drawers. Most children went barefoot to school, and a woman's one good dress might well be her burial garb, as was Nancy Tarbell's twenty-year-old black silk brought from Maine.

The people I write of are a microcosm of the development of the West. This story of the growth of the soil and the people who lived on it is an old, yet ever new story—one of courage and persistence as hard-working visionaries brought schools and churches, roads and houses, logging, shingle mills, sawmills, factories, grange chapters and farms to Columbia county. Let us be grateful for "this inexhaustible legacy."

Acknowledgments

In making my acknowledgments for help in the preparation of this book I pay my deepest debt and extend my warmest thanks to those anonymous local correspondents who sent their occasional notices to the newspapers of Columbia county. Often pedestrian and flat in presenting the unimportant, they were sometimes witty, even perceptive, and could, by a detail, give a clue to the important. They identified people, set the time for events, and reconstructed communities with their on-the-scene reports.

Old records are important. I have used real estate, marriage, court, school, church, grange and other records. Family records and documents, plus the memories of settlers older than I, have been checks against my own recollections.

I am indebted to the friendly helpfulness of countless unnamed persons in libraries, schools, churches, county offices, etc., and appreciate those generous families who assisted me. Both the Howard and Wilwerding families furnished me with much material and many photographs as they provided encouragement and approval for this project. Harry and Ethel Wilson also supplied several photographs for the book.

My thanks also to Dorothy and John Stofiel for the support of the Columbia County Historical Society, and to the Oregon Historical Society where many people helped me.

Quotations from various Tarbell letters used in the book are taken from *The Tarbells of Yankton* with the permission of the publisher, HaPi Press.

E.S.O.

COLUMBIA COUNTY HISTORY

Volume 21   1982-83

Officers of Columbia County, Oregon, Historical Society

President . . . . John Tomlin
Vice President . . . . Luanne Mathews
Secretary . . . . Jenelle Wysong
Treasurer . . . . Dorothy Stofiel

Directors
Shirley Nelson . . . . John Stofiel

Curators, County Museums
Billie Ivy . . . . St. Helens
Dorothy Stofiel . . . . Vernonia

Columbia County Historical Society Museum
511 East Bridge St.
Vernonia, Oregon 97064

Saving Old America for the Young

The Society has twenty volumes of county history, 1961-1981, for sale at the museums, or from the address above, for $2.00 each.

Contents

Special ten-page photo section on
early Columbia county logging and mills
follows page 142

Map #1

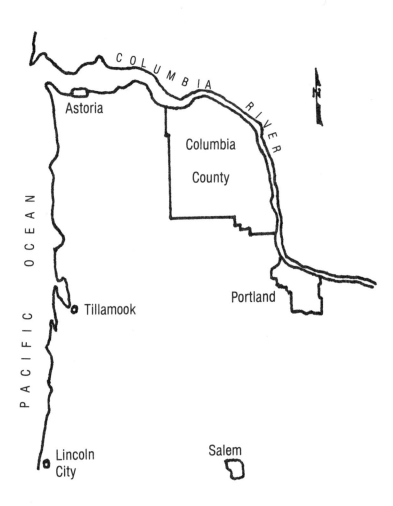

Columbia county, in Northwest Oregon, was established in 1854, having earlier been a part of Washington county.

I: OPENING THE INTERIOR OF THE COUNTY

A steep wilderness, whose hairy sides
With thicket overgrown, grotesque and wild,
Access denied; and overhead upgrew
Insuperable heighth of loftiest shade,
Cedar, and Pine, and Fir, . . . a Silvan Scene.

Milton, *Paradise Lost* (abridged)

Bunker Hill was waiting to be sheared of its covering of lush forests. Bunker Hill is not a hill or a mountain but a succession of rising undulations and ravines, ridges grown thick with forests, drained by rivulets which eventually meshed together into four different water systems. The higher ridges reach elevations of eighteen hundred feet in a region of ample rainfall. The springs and creeks of the many ravines flow into the Nehalem river, the Clatskanie river, Scappoose creek and Milton creek—the Milton creek tributaries forming the larger drainage basin for the Bunker Hill range. The Nehalem flows westerly into the Pacific, the Clatskanie northerly into the Columbia, Scappoose creek southeasterly into the Willamette slough, while Milton creek more leisurely winds its way through the hills, ending by going eastward into Scappoose bay.

Milton creek begins its meandering course five miles west of the Yankton school at an elevation above a thousand feet. Beginning as a mere creeklet flowing from a spring it gains reinforcement from a hundred trickling streams as it follows its leisurely course, first northward for as much as five miles, rounding the higher hills in making a large bend back toward the southeast. Thus it makes a ten mile journey to gain two miles on its easterly course.

Below the Yankton school Milton creek is joined by Tedford creek which rises from a spring only a few yards from the Milton creek source. Tedford creek flows steadily eastward while the more leisurely Milton creek makes its longer journey around hills. From the juncture with Tedford creek, Milton creek winds its snakelike way easterly until five miles later it empties into Scappoose bay and so joins the Columbia river. A map of Milton creek shows its course to be roughly similar to a question mark on its face, with the base in Scappoose bay.

The watershed of Milton creek covers some thirty sections of land, thirty square miles of undulating hills. As one stands on Robinette road above the Yankton community and looks to the south and west he sees ridges rising in series one above another, all showing the uneven etching of treetops as the evergreens still cover the hills. Milton creek picks up more streams than one can name, but it takes in Apilton, Salmonberry, Smith, Tedford, Cox, Dart—each with its own system of tributaries.

The Milton creek watershed of gently pillowed landscape was ideal for forests. Nowhere in its area is the land flat, and rocky outcroppings are few. Firs, cedars, and hemlocks grew in abundance and to great size in the deep soil of these hills, watered by rainfall spread over most of the year.

To this fabulous timber the settlers from the timbered northland of Maine came, late in the 1870s and during the '80s and '90s — the interrelated Corliss-Briggs-Howard-Emerson families and others looking for timber land or farming land.

These families came out of the Maine forest country where generations had been turning the Maine woods into lumber. When Henry Thoreau made his first trip to the Maine woods in 1846 he heard that in 1837 two hundred and fifty sawmills on the Penobscot and its tributaries above Bangor had sawed two hundred million board feet of lumber annually. Some of the children of those lumber workers were headed toward Milton creek.

The development of the Milton creek valley and the

interior of Columbia county thus began in Maine when these timber workers felt the lure of Oregon timber.

The sixty-one people making donation land claims in Columbia county under the acts of Congress providing land for early settlers all elected to take their land along the Columbia river or Willamette slough or the lowland along the waterways. From the Scappoose area to the lowlands north of Clatskanie, land was claimed by settlers whose family names became embedded in the history of the county. Watts, Jackson, Poppleton, Miles, Lamberson were family names in the Scappoose area. To the north were claims by Laffer, Foster, Fowler, Fullerton, Posey, Achilles, Cooper, McKay, Brogli, Goring and Captain Knighton — who dreamed of making St. Helens the great town on the river. Caples had the same vision for Columbia City. The Merrills settled in Deer Island. On down the river were North, Warren, Vorhees, Plympton, Dobbins, Weed, Piper, McLane, Barr, Waggoner, Hill, Hodgkins, Hastings, Bryant, Bohnert. Not one of the claimants ventured into the interior of the county.

Into the 1860s only tentative wagon trails and scattered logging had edged up the Milton creek valley for a mile or two. The Perry farm a mile inland, where Francis Perry had built a sawmill on Perry creek, was an outpost. Perry had fallen trees, sawed lumber, and planted fruit trees. His pattern for the valley was not unnoticed by the coming settlers.

The Corliss family had a long and rich lineage behind George Corliss, the Puritan, who landed in Massachusetts in 1639. Not to tarry on the intervening generations, George's great-grandson David, born about 1756, was one of the early pioneer settlers in upper Maine, facing the wilderness where the forest came down to the sea. Marrying when about forty-two years old, he fathered eight children. One of them, Willard Murray Corliss, born August 5, 1805, in Cherryfield, Washington county, Maine, lived his life on the edge of the Maine woods and was known as a great hunter.

He not only killed 130 bears; he married a beautiful and charming New Brunswick nineteen-year-old lass, Elizabeth

3

Segee, and the two of them produced eight children. Although Willard Corliss remained in Maine to die at Smyrna, age eighty-seven, many of his children and grandchildren went west, for gold, for lumbering, for farming. The first child of Willard and Elizabeth Corliss was Maryann, born in 1831 in Smyrna, where in pioneering fashion she at age eighteen married Joel Hamilton Howard, who was also descended from a line of pioneering ancestors.

Maryann and Joel Howard settled in a two-story frame house in the village of Lineus in the south of Aroostook county. It was logging and timber country. Maryann gave birth to Willard Henry in 1851, Herbert Orville in 1853 and Laura Edna in 1855. Maryann, the mother, died in 1859. Herb Howard remembered standing on the stairway looking at the coffin as it was carried from the house and put on a lumber wagon for the ride to the cemetery. Even though Herb was six years old he was groomed in a red dress, his dark hair in curly ringlets. He had a fierce independence in his nature, an independence which he demonstrated in an early encounter when he first started in the country school. The school mistress set out to punish him for some slight mischief. He flung himself onto the floor and with flailing arms and legs got away from the teacher and ran from the room. He never returned to that — or to any — school. When a grown man he could neither read nor write his own name.

The rebellious young Herbert was not on easy terms with his step-mother. He began working in the Maine woods in his early teens and at the age of nineteen took a wife. The story in the Howard family is that the couple had a child, which did not survive, but the Maine records are inadequate to verify or dispute this well-established family belief.

The Maine archives do furnish a comment on this first Herbert Howard marriage.

On February 7, 1876, a deputy sheriff of Aroostook county filed a bill for $5.06 for thirty-eight miles of travel, one way, in serving a summons on the "within named libelee" and giving into her hand a copy of the attached libel. This word *libel* and its derivatives are used in the archaic legal sense of publishing a document or instituting a suit at law. The document which the deputy sheriff served on Mrs. Herbert Howard was signed Herbert O. Howard, though Herbert at that time did not write even his own name. The document tells its own story.

"To the Honorary Justices of the Supreme Judicial Court next to be holden in Houlton within and for the county of Aroostook on the last Tuesday of February 1876.

"Herbert O. Howard of Sherman in said county of Aroostook respectfully libels and gives this Honorary court the informed (sic) that he was lawfully married to Emeretta F. Gilman now residing in said Sherman on the 19th day of October, 1872. That ever since his said marriage he has always treated his said wife as a faithful and affectionate husband, but the said Emeretta wholly unmindful of her marriage covenant and duty refused to attend to the wants of your libellant and would abandon his home for several days at a time leaving nothing cooked for him *to eat* and on the 18th day of July 1874 abandoned and deserted your libellant and has utterly refused to live with him since though he has frequently requested her to do so. Wherefore your libellant prays that the bonds of matrimony may be severed between him and the said Emeretta as the same would be reasonable and proper conduce to domestic harmony and consistent with the peace and morality of society." Herbert O. Howard

This pleaded action, Libel 475, Howard vs. Howard, was apparently granted by the honorable court, for Herbert Howard was soon after this time married to Abbie Emerson in Lineus.

Abbie was the third child, first daughter of Charles and Elmira Emerson, both of pioneering families. Herb Howard was a man of action. He turned his eyes toward Oregon and headed west alone, leaving his pregnant wife to follow as soon as he found a place to settle. He went by train to San Francisco and worked for a short time in California before taking a boat to Rainier. Abbie followed his route, arriving in Rainier, met by her husband, in time to give birth to her first son, Calvin Fay Howard, born in Rainier August 14, 1877. A daughter Lizzie was born to the Howards on February 2, 1879. Two more children, a boy always spoken of as Herbie, and a girl Rhoda, were born at Rainier, both dying while young from an epidemic. Abbie herself died at Rainier August 8, 1883, and was buried in the Germany Hill cemetery near Goble, as were her two children.

Herbert Howard was only one of the number of Maine loggers looking toward Columbia county timber, with the Columbia river offering an easy way to get logs to mills. Herbert A. Corliss, Charles S. Emerson, and Charles H. Briggs—all related to Herbert Howard by matrimonial ties, all with their families—came to Columbia county near the same time.

Almira "Mira" Hooper was born at Machiasport, Maine, January 29, 1836, and married Charles S. Emerson March 14, 1854. They were the parents of eleven children: Everett; Frederick, who was to marry Mrs. Minnie Peterson in Yankton; Abbie, Herb Howard's wife; Alexander; George; Winnie, who married Leslie E. Bailey in Yankton; Charles; Mary; Frank; John; and Jennie. When Mira Emerson died November 5, 1889, five of her children had preceded her in death; six of them and her husband survived her.

Herbert Alvader Corliss came to Columbia county in 1877 to work in logging and dam building. He bought 320 acres of timberland from the state school lands in the upper Nehalem river area in 1883 and began his own logging operations. Corliss appears in various ways in the development of the valley. He logged at times with Howard or with Charles Briggs and in 1891 he was logging on Milton creek with Walter Sweetland, whose son soon married Tina Gray. When the sawmill started operating on Dart creek it was listed under the name of Howard-Corliss Lumber Company, though it soon became Herb Howard's mill.

In 1889 Corliss deeded 320 acres of land to his wife Celia E., a widow whom he had recently married in St. Helens, "in consideration of love and affection and $1.00" He bought at a foreclosure auction in 1891 a quarter section of good Milton creek land for $1705 in gold coin. At that time he had a well-developed country home on Milton creek near the schoolhouse which was later to be the Yankton school. Alice Tarbell Brown, newly arrived from Aroostock county, Maine, in the summer of 1891 wrote of the Herbert A. Corliss family home:

". . . the family I like best is the Herbert Corliss family. They have only been married a few years. Mr. Corliss came from Lineus but his wife who was a widow with a son and daughter was a Searsport lady of some culture, and a very nice person in every way. Her father and mother, Mr. and Mrs. Ridley, live with them and are a splendid pair of old folks. Mr. Corliss is a real smart man . . . They have a pleasant home, and *such* a garden. All manner of fruit, vegetables and flowers . . . Mrs. C. has I think fourteen different kinds of roses."

The Corliss orchard, the first in the area, was bearing fruit by 1885.

Two of the young Emersons were married and lived across the road from Alice Brown. She did not entirely approve of them — "these young people have no idea of getting ahead in the world" — but she wrote enthusiastically of the land on which they lived in a small but attractive house, "the simplest sort of cottage and unpainted," but decorated with climbing roses. "The cleared land is planted with apple, plum, and cherry trees and such bushes as gooseberry and currant. The farm has a well of splendid water and a good barn and sheds." Alice saw the farm as a desirable place for her father and mother to settle. Her description in 1891 indicates a farm established for a few years. Charles Emerson, the father, had bought the land from the Muckles in 1879 or 1880.

In 1892 Corliss sponsored a petition to the county court to have part of the St. Helens-Vernonia road declared a public highway, it "having been regularly traveled for more than ten years by the public as a public highway." The court so declared and set aside claims for damage entered by Herbert O. Howard and E. A. A. Crouse.

Herb Howard's younger sister, Laura, age sixteen, married Charles Henry Briggs in Houlton, Maine, on

September 21, 1871, and had a son Fred and daughter Annie born in Maine. Her husband Charles, anxious to get a foothold in Oregon, left Maine while Laura was pregnant with Annie. Thus the two brothers-in-law, Herb Howard and Charles Briggs, both left pregnant wives behind them as they headed for Oregon. Both wives followed soon after, Abbie Howard getting to Rainier in time for her delivery. Laura Briggs later took her new-born baby and her son Fred by train to San Francisco and by boat to Oregon. Their daughter Percie Mabel Briggs was born at Rainier in 1878.

Laura (Mrs. Charles Henry) Briggs, sister of Herbert Howard, and her son Fred and daughter Annie. Laura spent an active fifteen years in Columbia county, from 1877 until her death in 1892. This picture was probably taken in Maine before she left for Oregon.

Charles H. Briggs bought land on Milton creek from the Muckles in 1879 and established a logging operation on Milton creek where on January 13, 1883, he advertised in the *Oregon Mist* that he had taken up a stray steer. Inquiries were directed to Briggs Camp. It was here on Milton creek at what was eleven years later to be named Yankton that the fourth Briggs child, a daughter Alice, was born, in 1883.

Laura Briggs was upright in carriage and character, intelligent, witty, devoted. She was of slender build and attractive appearance. Her pleasant disposition and easy laughter combined with her generous spirit and helpful nature to make her a favorite. She, like her brother Herb, liked to tell stories of the family in Maine. She rode horseback easily and rode to the river towns for the family shopping.

In 1890 she brought her Aunt Rachael Corliss who had the "consumption," or tuberculosis, out from Maine so that the ailing aunt might have the advantage of a milder climate and be cared for. The Briggs were then at Pittsburg in the Nehalem valley. Laura contracted tuberculosis herself and died at the age of thirty-seven. Her brother Herb Howard was with her during her final days. The daughter Annie when not yet twenty also was afflicted and joined the other two in death. Charles S. Emerson conducted the funeral services for the three. Charles Henry Briggs, husband and father, donated land for the Yankton cemetery.

Laura was remembered by all who knew her for her sweet spirit and unselfish service to others. She took an active role in bringing a school to the area, organizing a voluntary school district which built a schoolhouse and opened a school in 1886, Laura being the clerk. It is understandable that for years the school was often referred to as the Briggs school.

The Muckle brothers settled on the Columbia river in 1874-75 with holdings in Rainier and St. Helens, but they also began securing land on Milton creek. The importance of water for logging in these earlier years cannot be exaggerated. Water was the essential element for the movement of logs. Three dams on Dart creek are mentioned over the logging years — dams built by Howard, Tarbell, and Kale for flushing logs down stream.

The importance of water and these dams is preserved in the record of land sales. Charles, James and Jennie Muckle sold 271 acres of land on March 21, 1893, for $4065 to James N. and William H. Brinn. The Muckles sold the land but reserved certain rights to give them logging access to land they still owned. They wrote into the document: "Reserving however the absolute and exclusive right to maintain and operate the water dams now in and across Milton and Tedford creeks on said premises together with the right to use said creeks and to use and divert the waters of same, without being responsible for the waste or damage to the banks of said creeks, or otherwise, also with the further right to overflow said conveyed premises without being held for damages therefrom. Also reserving to themselves all timber necessary for keeping the said dams in good order and repair; also further reserving all convenient roadways for ingress and egress from any portion of said premises." Milton creek and its tributaries had a network of dams for use in bringing logs to market.

Muckle had previously sold 38 76/100 acres of land from the same area to Rose A. Oliver, of Cowlitz county, Washington, on January 27, 1891, for $800, reserving the timber rights as well as the use of water: "Reserving however to the said grantor all the merchantable saw timber standing, lying, growing or in any other way being upon said premises together with the right to enter upon, build schutes, skid roads or other roads and to use all timber necessary for building, maintaining, and operating said schutes and roads for purpose of removing said saw timber or any part thereof from over, across and upon said described premises for the term of four years."

David C. Tedford, an unmarried man, bought lots in Columbia City in 1873, bought St. Helens property at auction for taxes from the sheriff James Dart for seven dollars in 1875, selling the lots in 1879. He also bought land along Tedford Creek, which he sold to the Muckles in 1881.

Tedford bought Rainier property from Henry Watkins in 1891 and became a prominent figure in Rainier development.

Dart creek took its name from James Dart, born in England in 1841, settled in St. Helens in 1866 to build the sawmill which the Muckles later bought. He was superintendent of the mill both before and after the Muckles bought it. He was sheriff of the county from 1872 to 1876, then county clerk for a term before returning to the mill superintendency. He owned land on Dart creek.

The Muckle brothers, James and Charles, bought timbered land on Milton creek in 1878, 1879, and several parcels in 1882. They were assuring logs for their sawmill on the Columbia river. On September 13, 1890, they sold to George A. and Mattie Massie 80 acres of land for $1650, reserving the right to cut the standing saw timber for four years. When the Massies sold the same 80 acres to G. L. (Lawrence) Tarbell on September 10, 1892, for $1900, the reservation of the timber for the Muckles was a condition of the sale, along with a right of way to the dam on Emerson creek. (This Emerson creek mentioned in the transaction may be what is known as Dart creek.)

Charles Briggs and Herb Howard, having worked for a time in the Rainier area, settled in the interior of the county. They bought eighty acres on Milton creek on April 3, 1879, paying $75 down and agreeing to pay $245 in two years at 10% interest. They soon were buying further tracts of timber land along the creek from the Muckles.

Charles Brigg's wife Laura died in 1892 in Pittsburg, and in March, 1895, he married Mrs. Josephine Corliss. He opened a general store at Yankton in 1896, giving up active logging.

Herb Howard was an experienced logger. As soon as he had saved enough money after landing in Oregon he bought oxen and began his own logging. He began working on Milton creek early in the 1880s, one of several small logging operators along the creek.

The logging followed established patterns, the fallers perched on their pinchboards several feet above the ground,

11

chopping and sawing until the giant tree fell. The tree was then bucked into lengths depending on the diameter of the tree and the capacity of the sawmill for which it was destined. With the fallen tree bucked into lengths the oxen came into play in getting the logs to water.

When a section of land was to be logged, a skid road was laid out according to the slope of the land. The planning of this operation required skill and experience. Skid logs were grooved and set at intervals of five or so feet to provide the proper skid for the heavy logs. With three or four yoke of oxen working together, three or four or even five sections of logs could be chained together by dogchains. Some photographs of logging operations clearly indicate the methods used.

An account book kept by Howard beginning in May, 1887, gives various sidelights on his logging operation and on the community. He was providing board for the men logging with him. On May 16 he bought an order of goods from the Gillton store of James Bacon for $22.80. In July he paid cash to Garison for cow killed, milk, butter, and eggs, $6.80. He was buying some materials for his workers and keeping a rough account of what they were getting in such advances: 1 pair of boots $4, one pair of calf boots $5, two pair of sox $.90, tobacco in various amounts at $.50 a plug, two pair of drawers $3.50, two shirts $3.35. Board was $2 a week. Beef cost 7 or 8 cents a pound, butter $.70 for two pounds.

C. Daggett worked for Howard and Wikstrom 59½ days and had a balance due him of $58.65. He worked for Howard for 10½ days. Daggett boarded with Howard in April and May, 1887; but in January, 1888, Howard was boarding with Wikstrom.

The account book in various ways indicates that Howard, over 1887, 1888 and 1889 gave employment to Daggett, A. Emerson, E. Emerson, F. Emerson, Joseph Stevens, C. Marsh, C. Miller, Stanwood, J. R. Sherman, Jesse Hendricks, Jesse Hendricks, Jr. (who received $1 a day, while men received $1.15), Henry F. Corliss, J. Switzer, Ridley, Sweetland.

In 1890 Wikstrom, Herbert A. Corliss and Howard seemed to be working some in partnership.

Howard's old account book, which at this writing is in the hands of Ira Howard, is a curiously revealing document, noting that Howard advanced Fred Emerson fifty cents worth of whiskey, and when Howard's cows went to the bull. Rosy went to the black bull on June 20th, thus was due on March 20. Nellie, Buc and Miles each went to the red bull. Even the sow got mention for maternal expectations on March 4.

Some notes in the account book could mean that Howard started his sawmill on his home farm on Dart creek in January, 1890. It was certainly a fully established mill with a boarding house when Frank Brown went to work there in January, 1891.

Howard's sawmill on his own land on Dart creek became a focal point for this lower Milton creek area. That land has been Howard farm for more than a hundred years, and at this writing Herb's son Ira Howard, with his wife, still lives in the spacious house built seventy years ago. Howard's mill and logging operation needed a few men; hence he had a small bunkhouse-boarding house and the record mentions various woman cooks working there. Alice Brown wrote that drunkenness was not permitted around the boarding house, but she also said that some of the men were "not very nice."

The Dart creek mill was supplied logs from Howard's own land or from logs cut up Dart creek. Dart creek and its own tributaries drained about five square miles of beautifully timbered sloping land. Howard had a millpond but he also had a dam for driving down his logs. Above his land was the farm the Tarbells bought from George Massie, the Columbia county sheriff, in the fall of 1892. Charles Tarbell wrote a letter on September 1, 1895, giving a glimpse into the kind of family logging prevailing up and down the Milton creek valley. It had been a dry summer, plagued by forest fires, and leaving a smoky atmosphere. "The boys," he wrote of his sons Lawrence and Bert, who were both men with families, "have got in about all the logs they can put in the stream till there comes rain . . . They got in about 40 in the last week they worked, which netted them about $100 . . . Lumber is advancing somewhat in price and the prospect looks somewhat better." This was small logging on a family farm basis. Up and down Milton creek and its tributary creeks other families, too, were cutting saw timber, some with more ambitious operations. Milton creek was the main artery for getting these logs to market, and through the 1880s and 1890s and into the 1900s, it was a busy thoroughfare.

Abraham A. Crouse came to Milton creek from Aroostook county, Maine, for a look at the big trees in 1891 and brought his large family of boys out in 1892 to begin logging operations on the creek. The big trees never ceased to amaze these Maine loggers. "I know it's a lie, but I have seen them," Crouse would say to his relations still in Maine. Alice Brown was awed by them. "You grow dizzy trying to see where the tree stops and the sky begins," she wrote, and she comments on the stumps from four to seven feet across. Much of the more accessible timber had been cut out by 1891.

Various small logging operators got their logs to the main stream by using dams on the tributaries and then when the season and water were right, combined crews of men worked Milton creek together. Major runs down the creek usually came following a good period of rain, November and February being favorite times for very large runs, when a million and more feet of timber could be washed out of the hills in a harvesting rush. Early in the morning of the chosen day the floodgates of the main dam on the creek would be opened and the foaming, churning water would hit the various piles of logs with a roar. The men working the banks had to be agile and wary, for the water tossed logs about in reckless abandon. Sometimes a jam could not be broken, and half a million feet of logs might be piled up to await another try when the dams were again full. A million board feet of logs may not mean much in quantity, but imagine the lumber for a hundred homes rushing down the stream in this roar of water, with a few men along the creek struggling to keep the logs from jamming up. It was a spectacular sight, and it was harvest time for the logging crews. If the run was a big one and a successful one, four or five thousand dollars worth of logs might be washed out of the creek in one lucky day. The logs at various times over the 1890s were worth from $3.50 to $5 a thousand, delivered at the mill.

After being sluiced down Milton creek to Scappoose bay, logs were separated out by the owners according to brand marks, rafted together and towed to the purchasing mill. Boom men with their calk shoes and long pikepoles were an essential part of the timber harvest.

The Howard Mill was small enough to be moved where logs were available to it. It began operation on the Howard farm on Dart creek, but in the mid 1890s it was moved to Bachelor Flat for operation and then after a year or two returned to Dart creek. In 1901 Howard found that he could have easier access to timber in the area southwest of Rainier near Stehman. He took his sawmill there, where he operated it for a decade, moving it once from near Fern Hill into Beaver valley. He did most of his own logging, and continued to use oxen, even when other logging operators, including Simon Benson, were using donkeys and railroads.

II: THE EXTRAORDINARY HERB HOWARD

A powerful man in his prime,
Stoutly he strode about on stalwart legs;
. . . free was his speech
And he seemed in good sooth a suitable man
To be prince of a people with companions of mettle.

Sir Gawain and the Green Knight

Herb Howard was one of the Maine timber-working pioneers to stay with logging and mill work and make a career of it. He was known as Herb Howard the sawmill man, honest, dependable, energetic, dedicated. He was himself a hard worker, and he was a hard driver. An accomplished bullwhacker, getting the most possible out of six or eight oxen, he also expected people to work. His word was his bond, and he wanted from those working for him honest labor.

After opening his own sawmill on Dart creek when he was thirty-seven, for more than two decades he ran sawmill operations, showing great ability and resourcefulness in dealing with the uncertain times. Starting his business work as an illiterate he taught himself to read and write and of course he became adept at numbers. If all reports of him are dependable, he loved to see his property accumulate. He took pride in being a "self-made" man, and like many other self-taught individuals, he remained scornful of "education" and critical of schooling. He could whack a bull's rump and get good work out of it without going to school.

Herb Howard's character undoubtedly mellowed over the years as he gained some substance. He was a person whom different people read differently. Alice Tarbell Brown gave us one glimpse of him in 1891. He allowed no drunkenness around the boarding house, she said, and continued, "Howard who owns the mill is a rough man and his wife wholly uncultivated but both are kind hearted and most neighborly. Mr. Howard will do anything to oblige a person he likes and he happens to like Frank very much and seems determined to offer us every inducement to live here." Alice went cherry picking with the wholly uncultivated Mrs. Howard one day at Perry's cherry orchard.

This Mrs. Howard was Herb Howard's third wife. Mary Ellen Hendricks, known as Molly, was born in 1869, daughter of Mr. and Mrs. Jesse Hendricks. Molly, 18, married Herb Howard August 14, 1887. She had a son for Howard, named Harry Orville, in 1888.

The summer of 1892 was a memorable one for Herb Howard. The *Oregon Mist* gave details involving him. June 3: "Mr. H. O. Howard who was so seriously hurt two weeks ago in his sawmill on Milton creek is reported as having regained consciousness and slowly improving at the hospital in Portland." June 24: "Mr. Howard is shipping from one to two carloads of lumber per day . . . . Our old friend H. O. Howard is still improving with the exception of his eyesight which the occulists think he will lose."

In July Howard's mill was furnishing 25,000 board feet of lumber to build the bridge over Milton creek, receiving $8.25 per thousand board feet for the delivered lumber. July 1: "Mr. H. O. Howard of Milton creek who suffered the loss of an eye some time ago by having a splinter from a circular saw driven into his head three inches, and who was pronounced hopeless by the physicians, is again at his post of duty, looking as well as usual except for the scar under his eye." Later in the month appeared the notice: "My wife, Mary Howard, having left my bed and board without just cause or provocation, I will not be responsible for any debts contracted by her. H. O. Howard, dated this 20th day of July, 1892." Mrs. Howard was at Carico, with the Hendricks or working out, and was reported "quite ill" in June.

On August 29, 1892, in the circuit court of Columbia county Mary Ellen Howard filed a complaint asking for a divorce and setting forth her grievances against Howard. She affirmed that she had been "a good, kind, loving, true, affectionate and dutiful wife," while her husband, from a few weeks after their marriage had treated her in "a cruel and inhuman manner," a generalization which she particularized.

Since about August, 1888, she said (which was one year after her marriage), Howard had called her a whore and falsely and maliciously accused her of having criminal intercourse with other men.

Howard on various occasions, she said, called her "a damned lazy good-for-nothing bitch," once over a dog, once because his sheepskin saddle blanket was mis-placed, once because she had gone "one afternoon, after she had gotten through dinner, to call on her mother for a few minutes only . . . called her a damned bitch, a damned whore and falsely and maliciously accused her of having been out to meet other men than him . . . and struck her and kicked her severely." She mentioned other occasions where she said Howard had struck her with a rope or his hand or had kicked her behind or threatened to use a switch on her.

Aside from giving a picture of an inharmonious marriage, this deposition contained an estimate of Howard's wealth at that time. Molly, in asking for damages for slander and alimony, estimated Howard's assets as land holdings, $6,000; sawmill machinery and fixtures, $4,000; horses, cattle, wagons, logging tools and others, $2,000; and "that she is informed and believes he owns other property, both real and personal, of which and the value of which is to her unknown."

She asked for $45 a month during the court action, $5,000 alimony settlement, $2,000 damages for the slanders to her name, and $100 attorney fees.

The court granted her a divorce in September. Divorce was not unusual in Oregon, even in the 1890s. Oregon listed 2,110 marriages during 1891 as against 458 divorces. Mary was restored in her maiden name of Mary E. Hendricks, was granted $100 lawyer fee and costs of the trial, $500 in cash and custody of her son Harry until further order of the court.

Molly was not too despondent over the bad name Howard was giving her. She was up Milton creek at Carico working for Mrs. Scott when she filed her deposition and in mid-September Yankeetown residents noticed "the smiling faces of Mrs. H. O. Howard and her sister Miss Hendricks, passing through our district" on the way to St. Helens to a dance. Both the sisters were "becomingly dressed in white with black sashes." Herb Howard went up to Carico to get his four-year-old son Harry for a weekend visit in October, and he took his daughter Lizzie to Carico for a dance on December 2. Both of the Hendricks sisters were married that January, Molly to Thomas Holstein, Annie to J. N. Brinn.

Herbert Orville Howard, his son Calvin, born August 14, 1877, and his daughter Lizzie, born February 2, 1879. The two children were born in Rainier, Oregon, to Abbie Emerson Howard, who died in 1883.

What kind of person was this Molly Hendricks Howard Holstein who described herself as "a good, kind, loving, true, affectionate and dutiful wife," and who was described by Alice Brown as "wholly uncultivated?" A picture of her was taken after her divorce from Howard, while she was Mrs. Thomas Holstein. When Herb Howard would drive his load of lumber past the house in which she lived she would go out by the road, waving her apron, cursing Howard and calling him vile names until he was out of hearing distance of her loud voice.

Herb Howard then married Mamie Taylor, who as a girl lived in Stayton, Oregon, and later taught school in Oregon City. Mamie gave birth to twins who died at birth. The story in the family is that the twins were buried in the orchard on the farm just east of where the farmhouse still stands. Mamie died November 2, 1896, of tuberculosis.

On December 16, 1899, at his Yankton home, Herb Howard married Lucy Jane Stehman, his fifth wife. Lucy was born at Woodland, Washington, on October 13, 1871, of a pioneer Oregon family of Pennsylvania Dutch descent. Lucy was twenty-eight at the marriage, more mature than had been any of the four Howard wives who preceded her. Lucy had lived among loggers at Stehman, out from Rainier, and she had cooked in camps. She was described by one of her daughters-in-law as being very easy-going. That probably means that she took life as it came, rolling with the punches. She proved to be durable, living until March 23, 1953. If Howard had manhandled any of his former wives, he did not Lucy. Lucy was from the Butts family on her mother's side, Oregon ox-team pioneers, as were the Stehmans. Some Butts families were early settlers in the Milton creek valley.

Lucy and Herb had nine children, seven of them boys: Herbert O., born December 26, 1900, died in 1903; Miles S., born May 28, 1902; Perry E., born October 3, 1903; Ira Thomas, born December 2, 1904; Josie Lucille, born May 16, 1906, married Jack Krettinger, took her own life, May 21, 1928; Joel Hamilton, born June 12, 1908; Charles Lewis, born June 18, 1910; John Franklin, born January 16, 1912; Laura, born June 10, 1915.

Thus Herb Howard, with children by each of his five wives, had seventeen children, six of whom died in early childhood. Lucy outlived Herb by twenty-one years. She is reported to have told one of her granddaughters after his death that "Herb Howard was a devil!"

Lucy Stehman married Herb Howard December 17, 1899, and bore him nine children.

Herb was the kind of man who could keep a bear cub as a pet and raise it with pride, teaching it to dance with him. Herb enjoyed the sociability of the country dances given in people's homes or in new barns. Usually on Saturday nights and on special occasions someone was giving a dance. Herb, as his bear became adept at dancing, took the bear to these dances and would put on an act, dancing with it. But the bear came to maturity and its wild animal nature expressed itself one evening at a dance. It took a swipe with its paw at Herb's face, catching him beside the nose and tearing a gash in his cheek. The deep scar remained as a memorial of this episode. It didn't take any further evidence for Herb to decide that the bear had reached a dangerous stage.

Herb liked to talk. He was a good raconteur, and old-timers and his children have memories of his dramatic flair for incident as he told of early logging days in Aroostook county, Maine, or on Milton creek in Oregon. Shotgun Johnson, an old bachelor, an authentic character, and a Howard cousin, who holed-out in a hovel on upper Dart creek where he ran range cattle, was in Howard's mellower older years a frequent visitor at the Howard home — for a free meal and for long gabfests. Language between the two was coarse and direct. They often raised their voices in disagreement, but they loved the metal and fire of this recalled expression of vigorous pioneer life. Shotgun Johnson never went to pay a social call on the Howards or even for his rare visit to the church on the hill without his shotgun slung under his arm. Often he had his feet wrapped in burlap gunnysacking or — in snowtime — walking on homemade boxlike snowshoes. But Howard liked Shotgun and welcomed his visits, ungrudgingly accepting his status as a freeloader at the family table.

Herb Howard was the most conspicuous man in the Milton creek area, having some land and timber holdings and a mill on the road. It was he who planked the public road for three miles and more from his mill to the railroad. Pedestrians blessed him for keeping their feet out of the mud. Settlers who drove over the new road were delighted with it. Everyone had an opinion on Herb Howard's character.

Ira Howard, Herb's son, was asked to comment on this question: Was your father stingy or thrifty? Ira gave a measured and extended answer.

"I'd say he was thrifty. He bought machinery and equipment for the farm and he kept it up. He looked ahead and acted. We had a large family, we used almost a forty-nine pound sack of flour a week. He used to buy his provisions at a place on Front Street in Portland. One day a salesman said to him, 'There's going to be a war, you better buy some supplies,' and he did. He bought a lot. He bought at least two tons of flour and a lot of sugar and lots of other supplies. He had that room there off the kitchen piled clear to the ceiling. Of course the war did come and we had flour and sugar when other people couldn't buy it. Visitors would come to our house and see white bread on the table when no one else had white bread. Stories went around about hoarding. He just bought a lot to be thrifty and prepared, even when there wasn't no war.

"He was patriotic. He bought ten thousand dollars in Liberty Bonds. He kept them piled in a big safe. He didn't have piles of gold in his safe as some people were telling around. He had a little gold, of course, but not much.

"I'll tell you a story about him and gold. People used gold in those days. They bought a team of oxen or a piece of land with gold. Herbert Corliss put down $1700 in gold pieces to pay for the land next to ours, land auctioned off. Well, when Molly, you know, got a divorce from Dad and he had to pay her five hundred dollars, he fixed up a trick. He wanted some fun for his money. He got a canvas bag and he filled it half full with big metal washers the size of twenty dollar gold pieces, metal washers that would clink and sound and look like gold in a bag.

"He put his five hundred dollars in gold in the top of that bag with a separation under it. He took that bag and went to see Molly and he clanked the whole bag down on the table in front of her and he took the five hundred dollars out and gave it to her and he had most of his bag full of washers left. He clanked them good and loud on the table as he picked them up, as though he had a big bag of gold left.

"Molly, she could use rough language. She could talk to a bull-whacker. Dad says she began cussing him out for being a stingy deceiving cuss and she didn't stop cussing him until he was out of hearing. I guess she didn't even stop then. Maybe she cussed him for years. Dad had a lot of fun with his washers.

"Dad let Perry — he's my brother — and me when we were kids get all the milk we could from the wild cows after the calves had all they wanted. Perry and I would run those cattle in the barn and strip them after the calves ran with them. We'd get a little milk from each cow and we'd separate the cream. We'd sell the little cream we had when we got a can full to the creamery at Rainier, sending it down on the train. We'd get maybe two or three dollars now and then and when we got five dollars we'd take it up to Charley Brigg's store and he'd exchange it for a five dollar gold piece and we'd put it in the safe. When we got enough we'd get a twenty dollar gold piece. When the war came and everybody was talking about Liberty Bonds, Dad told us we better buy a bond with it. We bought a hundred dollar bond.

"Was Dad interested in having an education for his children? No. He was like lots of men of his kind. He couldn't read or write his own name until he was thirty. He taught himself. He said them college kids is only educated fools. All a man needed to know was readin', writin', and ciphering. Only one of us children went to college. Charley went to Monmouth and he was a teacher.

"I went to St. Helens to high school one year. It was at the end of the war. I walked all the way. Both ways. He made me wear them hobnailed army shoes, rough and heavy with horseshoes on the heels — you know what they were like. He said, 'Them chicken thin shoes people wear wouldn't last no time at all walking on that gravel road.' He made me wear them awful shoes. I wasn't dressed like other kids. I went one year and quit. I worked two years and I bought my own shoes and I went one more year. I only went to high school for two years.

"You know Dad had a sawmill that he moved down below Rainier. He moved the mill to where he could buy good timber land. He logged the timber to his mill with oxen, even when other people were using donkeys. Well, after ten years down there he got tired of running the mill and he sold it to a couple of men who had made some money in sheep. They didn't know anything about logging. Well, in two or three years they went bankrupt and my Dad had a mortgage on the mill and he took it back and he sold it again. He used to lift his head a little and maybe puff out his chest a little and say, 'I walked out of Beaver valley with a hundred thousand dollars.'

"It was then he built this big house. And he bought his first automobile.

"Would you say he was stingy? I think he was thrifty. He was a hard-working man and he expected hard work of others."

I told Ira that a man who as a boy went to the Yankton school with the Howards said the Howards had a reputation for being tough, a family not to get mixed up with. "I never set foot on their farm in five years," he said. "The Howard place was, to me, a strange island surrounded by friendly, or at least not unfriendly, farms and families."

"Well," Ira said as he studied this view of his family, "it wasn't that us boys was tough. It was our Dad. I've seen him run boys off our farm when they stopped in to play on Sundays or in the evening. Dad always worked hard, and he had no patience with wasting time. He wanted all of us to toe the mark. He knew how long it would take us to walk home from school and if we were half an hour late he wanted to know about it. He had his business and he tended to it. He didn't like other boys keeping us from tending to our own business, whatever it was.

"No, I wouldn't say my Dad or any of us boys was mean. We just had our way. He was hard-working, and people who did business with him found him honest. You had to be a tough, driving man in them days to handle a three or four yoke of oxen hauling a load of logs down a skid road. That was my Dad. He ran a sawmill working with his men. He knew his business and he tended to it.

25

"Did he drink much? He'd say not. Yes, he'd take a drink of hard liquor — straight. He used to say that he'd stop and take a drink with the boys and then go on about his business. He'd say that; but I remember when I was with him in the wagon outside the saloon I'd sometimes wait three or four hours — seemed like all day to a small boy. Yes, he'd take a drink. No, he never squandered his money. If he drank he knew how to handle it. He was tough and his money came from hard work.

"The opportunity was there. Timber land was cheap and easy to buy, but you only got money out of it by hard work in getting out logs and cutting lumber. My Dad was a hard driver and a hard worker. He went to work when he was a boy and he worked all his life."

Laura was Herb Howard's youngest child. People would say, "Herb is a tough old codger, but where little Laura is concerned he is soft clear to the core." Laura, in turn, would say fifty years after the death of her father, "I adored my father. I always did. Even when I was fifteen and he wouldn't buy me the clothes I needed, I adored him. He was for me a remarkable man."

Laura talked easily and without reservation about her father. "Was he stingy? Yes! Well, and no. He was sometimes very generous to other people outside the family. Once a Bachelor Flat woman had a baby and he loaded a wagon full of things — two of everything: two sacks of flour, two bushels of potatoes, two pigs — and took it over to her family. When people really needed something, if he liked them, he'd do a lot.

"For his own family, no. He was tight. He didn't like to buy clothes for us children. He didn't want us spending money. I quit school because I couldn't have clothes like the other children wore. If you asked him for a penny for a school pencil it was all right. If you asked for a dime you were in trouble. For the farm, for machinery, he'd buy what he wanted. For my mother, for the house, no. He wouldn't put electricity in the house when electricity came to Yankton. He wanted good food. We ate well at our house, but he wouldn't get things for my mother.

"He bought that automobile, a Matheson Silent Six, fire engine red. He was very proud of it. He had the first automobile west of the railroad tracks. There were only two or three in St. Helens. He never drove it. He never drove a car at all. Cal drove it. Once Miles and some of the boys took it out and got a little wild on a party. That was all of that. That only happened once. Cal drove the automobile. That old car sat in the old barn — one side of it was a machine shop for the farm stuff, the other was the slaughter house — for a long time after he bought another automobile.

"I guess my father was something of a woman chaser. At least there were a lot of stories going around. He brought a woman out from Maine to cook in his boarding house. When he was going to marry my mother Lucy he bought this woman a big house in Scappoose to use as a boarding house. That was, I guess, his way of telling her that was the end.

"When he had the sawmill down back of Rainier he had a woman down there. My mother got on the train and went down and found them together.

"Did my father drink? He didn't buy much, but he would drink. Aaron Kelley who kept the saloon in Houlton says Dad would sit in the saloon on Saturday night after he had paid off his men and let the men buy a drink for the boss one after the other, but he'd never buy drinks for the men. He'd stay there Saturday night as long as the saloon was open, letting his men buy him drinks — that's what Aaron Kelley used to say.

"When prohibition came to Oregon he quit drinking, just like that. He wouldn't pay the price for it. He didn't drink any more. Oh, once or twice he drank homemade wine. Once at a Portuguese affair—but that doesn't matter.

"He built a sawmill up at Apiary for his two sons Calvin and Harry. He wanted them to run it together, to be a three way affair. But it didn't last long. Harry was jealous of Cal and pulled out of it. Dad was always partial to Cal. Cal was his oldest son. He gave Cal ten acres of good land and lumber to build a house when Cal was married — all free. Harry was Molly's son. Molly raised him. He didn't see much of the Howards until he was grown. After the sawmill split he never came to see the Howards, but sometimes one of us would go see him.

"My Dad was over sixty when I was born. Soon after that he became sickly and wasn't able to work hard. I never knew him in his hard-working years. He had worked hard all his life. He made his way himself . . . his life was hard. He was hard. And tough. And tight. I adored him. I thought — I think — he was a great man, worth being remembered."

A lawyer who served Howard over many years called him "a very true, loyal and intimate friend" and said, "I had great admiration for his business ability and energy, his integrity and fair dealing with all men, and his excellent traits as a citizen."

Lawrence Tarbell, Howard's neighbor for forty years, thought well of him as a neighbor and citizen. When Herb died he had the biggest and most prosperous farm, and the biggest house, in Yankton.

III: ROADS

To haul produce on our dirt roads costs about 25 cents
per ton per mile, on Macadam roads 8 cents per ton per
mile, on railroads by trainloads and long haul under one
cent per ton per mile, ocean transport even less.
Report of the committee on good roads,
Oregon State Grange Proceedings,
May, 1906.

The *Oregon Mist* reported in March, 1887, that 138 claims
of 160 acres each were available in township 5 north range 3
west, the area on the upper Clatskanie river and the Milton
creek bend. These quarter sections of land were of good
quality, well watered and excellent timber land.

The difficulty of settling in this inner county was
inaccessibility. When Clark Parker entered the upper
Nehalem area from Washington county in the spring of 1874
he made his own trail through the woods and over the hills.
He marked out his homestead and built a split cedar cabin.
He brought his wife and children, Andy, Julia, George,
Knute, Pete and John in on foot and with pack horses. The
next year another son, Albert, was born. Henry and
Catharine VanBlaricom followed the Parker-blazed trail into
the valley and other settlers came along: Spencer,
Mellingers, Tuckers, Pringles, Weeds, Brouses, Cherrington. Settlers used pack horses and trails in from Washington
county.

Israel Spencer, a GAR veteran, went into the Nehalem
valley in 1876. He wrote two letters to his brother in
Michigan telling of his newly settled area. To get the stuff
we have to buy, he said, we use pack horses carrying 150 to

200 pounds each over an 1800 foot mountain. That meant over the top of Bunker Hill and down Milton creek to St. Helens. This trip "was not much fun, you bet." Five families that summer were living in the upper Nehalem river area, though other claims were being taken up. "One man came in yesterday and took a claim today."

Spencer said, "There is a pretty fair wagon road all the way but eight miles which we intend to cut through in the fall." His expectations were premature. It was not until 1879 that enough voluntary manpower was available to cut the road through the forest over Bunker Hill. This road connecting the inner county with the county seat was important, but getting a good road through from the county seat to the Nehalem valley remained a continuous problem for a generation. A violent storm closed the road in 1880 and it had to be reopened. The road went from the East fork of the Nehalem past Elkhorn Spring and along the ridge between Cox and Tedford creeks to the corner where the Yankton school was to be built.

Alice Brown had a first-hand comment on this road from that corner into St. Helens. "It is nearly all woods from here to the station and such trees! The wagon track winds in and out among them. In some places there are three tracks, often two running either side of a clump of these great trees." In wet weather these dirt wagon ruts became deep. At its best in good weather the road over Bunker Hill was a mere wagon trail.

Various conflicting accounts of the opening of that Bunker Hill road have been given. An unsigned account in the *Columbia County History*, volume 1, 1961, page 55 reported that about 50 men, working from Pittsburg east met a crew of men working from Yankton west at Elk Horn Spring June 9, 1879. William Pringle, one of the participants, had a quite different version in the *St. Helens Mist*, November 30, 1923. "It was in April, 1879, that fourteen of us Nehalem boys started out to build the road. We started at the Yankton end and the St. Helens people furnished the grub and we furnished the labor . . . Our party consisted of Peter, George and Jacob Brouse, W. S. Pearson, George Pearson, John

Daly, John and William Pringle, A. H. Matthews, Albert Tucker, Willard Tucker, A. H. Powell, Andrew Elliott and William Hazel; and one of the best spans of mules that ever a man drew lines over . . . .

"It took us a little more than two months to reach Pittsburg and when we did reach it the women of the valley had a big dinner prepared for us. I remember that Mrs. Martha Howell, Mrs. Kate Matthews and Mrs. Detrick had charge of the affair.''

Jacob George in the March 29, 1918 *Oregon Mist* gave his version of the roadbuilding. The men working the east or Yankton end of the road included the Muckles, the Georges, Tom Watts and several others. George said that he remembered the meeting with the Vernonia people, the Brouses, Parkers, Tuckers, Powells, and others.

Judson Weed in 1918 recalled the wind storm which closed the newly opened road in January, 1880. Trees blocked all the roads and trails into the valley and snow fell on the down trees. Those settlers in the valley had to live on what they had. Flour vanished and many were without bread for months. Weed lived in a log cabin and ground what wheat he had in a coffee grinder. Settlers worked six months to reopen a new road.

The Vernonia post office was started in 1876 in the house of David Baker, who was the postmaster. In 1879 weekly mail service was established between St. Helens and Vernonia, Joe Campbell carrying the mail horseback over the newly cut out road across Bunker Hill. He left St. Helens Friday at 8 a.m., stopping overnight at the W. S. Pearson home on the East fork of the Nehalem. By the fall of 1891, mail to the Nehalem valley was leaving Houlton on Tuesday, Thursday and Saturday.

The county commissioners might have been only partly sympathetic with the plight of inner county settlers who needed roads, for they were mostly from the river side of the county; but the commissioners had little resources with which to meet the needs of the county. The entire county tax in 1877 came to $6614.82, and even so, complaints were

31

heard of high taxes. It was many years before the county or any road district voted a road tax.

The coming of Henry Villard's Northern Pacific Railroad into the county in 1883 was a significant development. The Northern Pacific had built the railroad from Kalama, Washington Territory, to Tacoma between May, 1870, and December 11, 1873, starting from Kalama where a locomotive and materials were unloaded from an ocean steamer. The railroad received generous land grants to encourage its building. In 1872, two locomotives were engaged in the building along the Cowlitz. About 750 Chinese and 500 Caucasians were employed in this construction between Kalama and Tacoma. The railroad down the river on the Oregon side was planned to connect Portland and Oregon with the Puget Sound country.

The railroad brought the relocation of Scappoose when William West donated land for a depot and switching yard. The store and post office were moved from Johnson's Landing on the slough to the railroad line. Where the railroad crossed Milton creek became a flag stop called Milton with a box car on a siding in lieu of a depot. St. Helens was by-passed. Columbia City, already platted as a town and expecting to become a metropolis, was on the line which extended to Goble.

Henry Villard and a distinguished company of five-star guests, including ex-president Grant, were on the north bank of Deer Lodge river in Montana attending the ceremonies of driving the last spike to finish the railroad from Lake Superior to Puget Sound when Villard received the telegram informing him that the railroad between Portland and Goble was complete. It was September 8, 1883.

The ferryboat *Tacoma* was assembled in Portland from pieces cut in New York and shipped around the Horn. It was launched May 17, 1883, and was ready to transfer trains across the river in the fall. Thus train service between western Oregon and the Puget Sound country passed through Columbia county for many years before a railroad bridge spanned the Columbia river at Vancouver in 1908.

One traveler commented on the ferryboat ride over the river in 1889. "Our train went to Goble and on to a ferry boat to cross the Columbia river. It was thrilling to me to see the big boat settle down in the water with the weight of the cars and I thought sure we would sink."

In June, 1894, the Columbia river flooded. The passenger boats for St. Helens discharged passengers into the second story windows of Mr. Blakesley's hotel. Cattle and people had to be taken off Sauvie Island. Kalama was almost entirely under water. The Northern Pacific trains had to be taken onto the ferryboat *Tacoma* at Kelso and run into Portland on the boat. The train service was thus disrupted for a month before the ferryboat landings could be used at Kalama and Goble. Cordwood banked along the river was flooded away. Many fruit trees were killed by the flood. It was the highest water ever recorded on the river. Water was forty inches deep on the St. Helens post office floor.

And 1894 was not yet over for the county: five feet of snow fell in the Bunker Hill area. In January, 1895, Vernonia was flooded by the Nehalem river and Rock creek runoff. Milton creek had the greatest volume of water ever seen in it, flooding out a bridge or two.

The mud gave impetus to a move for a plank sidewalk from St. Helens to Houlton.

It was James J. Hill, the Empire Builder, the railroad man, who finally bridged the Columbia river with a railroad between Portland and Vancouver, and then not primarily to connect Portland with the Sound, but to connect the Port of Portland with the mid-West and East by way of the north bank water level rail route, through Spokane. Hill organized the Spokane, Portland and Seattle Railroad Company, spending forty-five million dollars to build the railroad. Eight million of those dollars went to build the three bridges over the Columbia river, the Columbia slough and the Willamette river.

Portland was set for a big banquet to celebrate the event, and railroad moguls from the northwest and east gathered with Portland commercial leaders to celebrate the crossing of the big river. The first passenger train to cross over the river carried Hill and numerous other prominent figures on November 5, 1908. Hill stood on the rear platform of the observation car as the train crossed over the Columbia, looking up and down the river. "Magnificent!" he said. "It is worth it."

The railroad men went on to Astoria, looking over railroad expansion possibilities, returning to Portland for the November 6 banquet at the Commercial Club, three hundred and fifty strong — all with their names listed in the *Oregonian* the next day. The program was long, closed by the witty sallies of Charles Erskine Scott Wood, after a rather dull address by James J. Hill and talks by a dozen others.

The trains from Portland to the Sound no longer needed to go through Houlton and take the ferry from Goble to Kalama. That twenty-five year venture in using the train ferry as a moving railroad bridge was ended. The *Tacoma* was moved to Puget Sound to operate there.

The railroad was a step forward in transportation, but the county was to slosh and struggle in muddy roads for many years before a system of road maintenance developed. More and better roads became the frequently reitterated cry. The first resolution passed by the first Columbia county grange meeting was a plea for roads. The editor of the *Oregon Mist* was merely expressing the common feeling when he wrote on September 18, 1891, that Columbia county needed roads and bridges, especially into the interior of the county, "ways by which a farmer can reach a market with his produce and by which new settlers can reach their claims — not by means of a packhorse — by good wagon thoroughfare."

The editor was also expressing the common sentiment when he wrote, "We want to reach out for home seekers . . . more people is what Columbia county is sadly in need of . . . . We have more good land subject to homestead entry than any other county in the state."

The nineties began with a feeling of hope and expectation for the five thousand people in Columbia county. The population had more than doubled in a decade and everywhere were signs of promising development. The

Oregon Mist, published in St. Helens, already eight years old, had a new publisher-editor, J. R. Beegle, who stated in various ways week after week, the gospel of optimism for the county. His New Year's message to his readers to begin 1892 was, "Indications are for progress in farming, lumbering, road building, railroad construction. Before the close of 1892 we earnestly believe that a railroad the entire length of the county, and to Astoria, will be completed." It was not completed until 1898.

A resident of Deer Island, in boundless enthusiasm, foresaw "a father city" in that location. "We possess all the requirements necessary for a large city — excellent water, unlimited timber, iron and coal, excellent transportation facilities, splendid manufacturing locations, and a good farming country to back it. The only direct and practicable route into the Nehalem and Clatskanie is from Deer Island."

The possibility of mining was in the air. A note in the *Oregon Mist*, October 30, 1891, sets the theme for development. "A party of experts from Portland and Oswego are now examining the iron mines of Bunker Hill with the idea of purchasing. It is to be hoped that steps will be taken to develop them when they are sold and not hold them as the iron beds on Milton creek are, simply to keep someone out who would improve the property and thereby benefit the county."

The editor of the *Oregon Mist* emphasized the need for roads for the farmer to get his product to market; but Columbia county was hardly agricultural at that stage in its development. It had in 1890, 385 farms with twenty thousand acres of farm land listed as "cleared," mostly dairying land.

The fragmentary records of those years near 1890 give some indication of both the importance of roads and the difficulties in travelling them. Omar Spencer, speaking on the hundredth birthday of Columbia county remembered that as an eight-year-old boy he and his father had driven a yoke of oxen, without any vehicle, from Vernonia to St. Helens in one day, going over the Bunker Hill road. He said that they sold the oxen for two hundred dollars. In the same year Elmer Everett Nickerson took two days to go from Cornelius to Vernonia, probably with a loaded wagon. A November, 1891, note said that the rains had made the road "almost impassable," and that expression *almost impassable* became a frequent qualification in remarks about the roads in wet weather. In December, 1891, a Carico resident reported, "The mud and water is nearly boottop deep between here and St. Helens."

An anonymous horseback rider made the trip from St. Helens to Clatskanie in February, 1892, writing a letter descriptive of the settlements along the way and the road he travelled. This important letter is in the February 26, 1892 *Oregon Mist*. "St. Helens is the only place on the route that has the appearance of a city. You have excellent paved streets and good sidewalks clear through the city. In Columbia City the road was recently slashed of brush. Here I saw an excellent schoolhouse, an old sawmill, a wood dock, a four-story hotel, some moss-covered tumbledown houses and some very neat cottages."

Deer Island, a new town in an excellent farming area, had only a few buildings — a general merchandise store, a saloon, an N.P. railway station. This, he said, was the business center for Tide creek logging.

Hunters was the old railroad transfer point. It had a sawmill and the Tide creek boom. Reuben had several buildings, a general merchandise store, saloon, wood wharf and warehouse.

Goble was the railroad transfer point. "The Northern Pacific has a fine depot here" and several buildings marked the town — a hotel, saloon, store and some houses. Goble was the shipping point for the large sawmill a couple of miles up Goble creek, with a capacity of 50,000 board feet a day. A double flume ran from the mill to the wharf. Twelve miles of flume carried lumber and cordwood and stave bolts.

Reuben was connected with the Nehalem valley by a wagon road. Neer City was a cordwood and timber town, with a large wharf, warehouse, store and several good residences. Danby had a sawmill.

Rainier "is a beautiful hamlet on a gentle slope." W. J. Muckle and D. C. Tedford were prominent citizens. Muckle and Co. had a large store and the town had several fine residences. Two or three sawmills, a sash and door factory, shingle mill and several small industries marked the town. North of Rainier was farming country.

Clatskanie was a new town. It had six sawmills, many neat cottages and fine residences.

In 1892, the road needed work done on it. Where it had heavy puncheon it was good, but some bridges were rickety and dangerous. Columbia county needed better roads and bridges.

This letter offering rare historical insight is unsigned.

An advertisement for a new stage line appeared in the *Oregon Mist* August 12, 1892, announcing a new era in travel, but the roads were still the same old roads.

"The Houlton and Vernonia Stage Co. are now running a daily line between Houlton and Vernonia, leaving Houlton every day except Sunday at 9:30 a.m. or immediately after the arrival of the north-bound train from Portland. It has hitherto been rather inconvenient traveling between the above-named places, but we now have the best accommodations, as this company has fine young horses and good comfortable riding stages. Rates $2.50 one way, $4.50 round trip."

The road from Houlton to Howard's mill on Milton creek was bad enough that fall for Howard with some help from neighbors to undertake the private planking of it. This planked road brought forth the comment when the October rains began, "This is the weather that makes the pedestrian bless the people who laid the plank road from Houlton to Maineville."

Roads are a subject of frequent mention in the paper, both from the editorial comment and from local correspondents. Occasionally a letter to the paper expresses the feeling of a concerned citizen. One such writer urged that dangerous road bridges in the county receive immediate attention "before the county is compelled to pay a heavy damage from accidents." A notice of the improvement in the railroad crossing at Houlton called attention to the difficulty in the crossing which had prevailed too long. "The hitherto steep incline has been so changed it is now possible for a team to draw an ordinary load over the track at that place."

The November 18, 1892 Carico valley news was that "News is scarce, rain is falling, the roads across Milton creek bottom are almost impassable."

The residents of Milton creek bottom took some private action to improve the public road. Two and one tenth miles of the road were planked with lumber from Howard's mill, 298,377 feet of lumber being used. Herbert A. Corliss took the lead in this community project and supplied 42 days of volunteered labor. Abraham Crouse worked 35 days and contributed three yoke of oxen for 11 days. Other men contributing lesser amounts were D. M. Corliss, J. Braddack, the blacksmith, C. C. Brown, Gordon C. Barger, Lawrence Tarbell, Charles H. Briggs, Frank Brown, Charles Brown (Frank's young son), N. A. Perry, Mr. Wright, Rudolph Kappler, Mr. McKay, Brinn brothers, B. I. Plummer. This added up to a total 199½ days of citizen volunteer labor, not counting the oxen, as reported by H. A. Corliss.

The bridge across Milton creek at Maineville was built in June, 1894, by Abraham Crouse.

The January-February weather of 1893 accented the difficult road problems for the Houlton-Vernonia axis, and particularly the upper Milton creek area of Carico and Peris. The area had a snowfall of about five feet, blocking the roads entirely for a time. "The mail from Houlton to Vernonia has not been making connection during the blockade. The latter city was for several days without mail communication, the carrier being unable to make the trip." As the snow began to melt, the reporter said, "We have made mention before of our roads being impassable, especially, the St. Helens and Carico road across Milton creek bottom."

The problem with the Milton creek bottom led some of the residents to undertake making a higher road around that section. The Carico reporter was only half convinced of the wisdom of such a move. "The new road from Carico to Yankeetown is said to be almost open. We think it is a very good idea to have plenty of roads through the county, but it would be better to put more work on the roads we now have than to undertake to build so many new roads through a part of the county that is not settled up and no prospect of its being done at present." Even into the summer and fall the news picked up the refrain — when it rains the roads are muddy and travel became difficult.

Snow began falling in the Milton creek bottom in early November. The promise seemed to be of another wet winter. "The people of this place (Peris) have learned there is no use making new roads and cut-offs to avoid crossing Milton creek bottom, so they are now corduroying the bad places." But a week later, "The heavy rain of Tuesday caused an overflow of Milton Creek, which did some damage to our public thoroughfare across the bottom." But more than rain and high water was damaging the road. The new corduroy was damaged by careless driving. "The man who went down the road last Wednesday driving an ox team and tearing out the corduroy ahead of him, would be thanked if he would put it back the way he found it." Apparently not all drivers liked the corduroy and something less than harmony prevailed in the upper valley.

To avoid the Milton creek bottom mud the adventuresome traveller might try the Bunker Hill road to Vernonia, but here, too, the reports were less than encouraging. In September, 1894, when the roads might be expected to be at their most usable season, this report under the heading "Over a Bad Road" appeared in the *Oregon Mist*. "Captain Geo. J. Ainsworth and party, who passed through St. Helens about ten days ago, met with no little difficulty on their journey toward Nehalem. When they reached Bunker Hill one wagon broke down and the party camped there until the vehicle could be brought back to St. Helens for repairs, which was done last Saturday. The road between this place and Pittsburg is said to be very rough, and to those familiar with it no surprise was expressed when it was learned the party was having difficulty."

The attempt to build a road around the creek bottom area moved forward. The Peris report, October 19, 1894, read: "S. Rock and C. C. Moyer have the new road opened out past the post office so that it can be traveled by horses and footmen and it is a better grade and seven rods nearer by measurement, than the county road. If we had a few more men such as Rock in this place we would have better roads, but we have a few mossbacks here who will not make roads themselves and do all they can to keep others from making improvements in that line." As an added endorsement the reporter adds, with little regard for grammar, "S. Rock has the largest spuds we ever seen."

Even though Moyer was engaged with Rock in the project of opening a hill road, he was still concerned over the bottom land road. The May 2, 1895 Peris report included the note: "The road across Milton creek bottom is in very bad condition, almost impassable. C. C. Moyer intends to soon commence improving the roads."

Winter weather renewed the problems of the Milton creek bottoms with roads. Most of the logging camps were shut down by the cold and snow. In mid-January a warm turn in the weather and rain combined to supply the greatest volume of water in Milton creek seen for years. The snow had been five feet deep. "The Houlton-Vernonia mail-carrier and some pedestrians had to lay over at this place (Peris) last Saturday and Sunday on account of Milton creek's overflow." C. C. Moyer was kept busy trying to keep wind-fallen trees clear of the county road, "which were put in by recent blizzards." Peris had an enterprising citizen who took advantage of the stoppage in travel to put out a sign "meals and lodging." Two notices in the Peris locals might have been written by the same reporter: "The county road from this place to St. Helens was never in better condition for winter than at present" (February 15, 1895), and March 29, "The roads across Milton creek bottom are in an almost impassable condition."

But by July 12 the road supervisor, who seemed to be Moyer, was receiving a pat on the back: "Our supervisor has done good road work this summer. Roads are best ever.'' However, when wet weather came, the tune changed.

The mail service into the inner county depended upon these unsure and difficult roads. At the early beginning of the mail route, the postmaster at Houlton, Mr. N. A. Perry, was reported as having trouble filling the contract for the position. As Yankton, Peris, and Carico developed post offices on the route and as the road situation improved a little with the advance of the decade, the pay for the mail route attracted attention. Peris lost its individual mail carrier in 1894 and that mail route was handled by the Houlton-Pittsburg-Vernonia carrier, ''A saving of $160 a year.'' This move followed closely the establishment of the Yankton post office. Houlton was soon expressing civic pride in being the mail distribution center for more than half the area of the county.

The contract to carry the mail the twenty-five miles from Houlton to Vernonia six times a week via Yankton, Valley, and Pittsburg (the Peris post office was closed at the end of May, 1901) paid $893.99 a year in 1901, but the new four-year contract made in February, 1902, paid $1399 a year.

A Yankton voice sounded a little dissatisfied with the development of the community. It was November and the wet season was affecting the roads again when this note appeared: ''Where, o where, is our new plank road? Yankton is somewhat noted for talking improvements which fail to materialize. Let us get on a little more steam.'' Roads in the valley as the century turned were still dirt roads, ungraded and rutted by wagon wheels, deep with mud or dust. The road Howard had planked from his mill to Houlton several years before had by 1900 long been worn out. It was back in the mud again. Corduroy and other fillers had been used over some of the worst-offending areas; but year after year the settlers and teamsters moving up and down Milton creek had a battle with the road. The county court began to appoint district road supervisors toward the end of the 1890s, but up to that time road work had been mostly labor contributed out of community need. Some accounts of payment for such labor begin during the decade to show up in the record of court expenditures, at last on the meeting of the court at the beginning of January, 1900, the decision was made to levy a tax for roads.

In August, 1901, the county bought a road grader for $325. It was an awkward contrivance mounted on four wheels pulled by horses. It did not prove to be very practical in use.

The county purchased its second road grader in March, 1902, a grader manufactured at Scappoose. The reporter said that "these machines have been used with good results in many places." The machine was used on the Houlton-Yankton road when the fall rains were set in and in December the road was in "awful condition." It is understandable that some farsighted citizen should begin making a plea for the county "to acquire a small portable rock crusher for road improvement." Run by a twelve to fifteen horsepower engine, he said, such a machine could be acquired for from two thousand to twenty-five hundred dollars. However, rocking the dirt roads of the county was to come only slowly.

In January, 1903, the county court awarded S. Rock a contract to construct 1¼ miles of new road near the C. C. Moyer place on upper Milton creek, getting the Vernonia road partially out of the Milton creek bottom mud. The new road, to cost $199, was to be corduroyed, indicating that crushed rock was still in the future.

The county acquired a small portable rock crusher by the spring of 1904. The *Columbia Register* could report on June 17 of that year that "the supervisor expects to make at least 1¼ miles of permanent road this year." A mile and a quarter of road would not go very far in the county with all its back country dirt roads, but it was a beginning. One might raise the question of how permanent a "permanent road" is, especially a rocked road over a clay base when teams are trucking lumber. But the county at last had both a grader and a small rock crusher. In December, 1905, the county court agreed to crush rock for the road in Houlton, then incorporated, if the city would pay for putting it on the road. "The town can do no better than accept the proposition."

In March, 1906, the rock crusher was taken to Clatskanie to crush rock for a piece of road there. "The more places the rock crusher visits the better it will be for the roads of Columbia County," conceded the *Oregon Mist* writer. But naturally the question of priority was always urgent. When the road between Houlton and St. Helens was rocked, the cry was that it would have been better to rock the road from Houlton west toward Pittsburg, "at least as far as Franz Hill," a distance of a mile or so. That road took a lot of heavy lumber and wood and shingle hauling, with ten teams hauling lumber from the two Milton creek lumber mills.

In early December, 1906, a road meeting for the Milton creek-Houlton district was held at the courthouse. It was voted that a 6 mill tax for road work be levied. The committee of Dr. Edwin Ross, Lawrence Tarbell and G. W. Perry proposed that the county court improve the Houlton-Yankton road and grade it, covering the road with crushed rock at least to the top of Franz Hill, at an estimated cost of $900. The editor of the *Oregon Mist* wrote, "The action of the people of road district 3 in voting a special levy of 6 mills and designating the manner in which the money was to be expended was wise and timely." The committee also asked to have the road over the hill by the Yankton church cut down, also at a cost estimated to be $900. It was to be several years before this work was finally done.

But the county was at last started in the direction of road improvement on a more permanent basis than such patch work as planking and corduroying. But even so, Yankton was to see another plank road built before it was to see any crushed rock road.

Changes, improvement, were in the air. The Houlton barber shop advertised that its patrons who wanted baths could now use a porcelain tub! The Bank of Columbia was established in St. Helens.

The railroad company finally agreed that the ten by twelve station they had built eighteen months earlier was too small, and built for Houlton a larger station.

43

"We hear that H. O. Howard is contemplating building a handsome new home on his farm of 300 acres. He has several men working and putting the land under cultivation." Herb Howard built the new home and it still stands. Dr. Ross built a very comfortable summer residence on his farm on upper Milton creek and "rusticated" there with some of his St. Helens friends, notably the family of W. B. Dillard.

Lou Barger returned to Yankton to work in the Masten camp and built a new cottage which "is quite an addition to the town." Robert Jeffries built a home next to Barger's. Christ Jensen was preparing to build. "Watch Yankton grow."

In October, 1909, the reporter could at last say, "since the roads between here and Houlton have been put in such good condition, we feel quite near to the metropolis, St. Helens." Possibly that was before fall rains, for the road was not yet rocked.

A more buoyant feeling regarding the roads was emerging. The *Oregon Mist* commented on the Houlton-St. Helens road: "When Jack DeSpain gets the mile of road from Houlton to St. Helens finished it will be fit to run a baby wagon over without waking the kid, and it will connect with an excellent road to Bachelor Flat, Yankton, Warren, Scappoose, Deer Island, etc. St. Helens is the center of a rapidly expanding system of good roads that will before many years extend to the Nehalem valley and there should be no let-up until this is accomplished." The roads were largely still ungraveled, but there was agitation for the county to develop its own quarry and increase rock crusher capacity.

In November: "quite a number of teams are seen on our road lately hauling lumber and shingles from the mills." The Yankton notes for May 13, 1910, set the new tone: "The farmers of Yankton are very busy preparing their land for potatoes and other crops. The shingle and sawmills are manufacturing lots of shingles and lumber, but none are more busy than the ladies of Yankton assisting mother hen in taking care of her chickens."

The new Herb Howard house (built in 1910) and his new automobile. This was Howard's first automobile. In front seat are Calvin Howard and wife, daughter and step-daughter. Herb Howard is in back seat with four of his children.

The July 14, 1911, *Oregon Mist* carried an editorial note: "Last Sunday a large number of automobiles from Portland were in town and the groves along the Portland road were used as picnic grounds . . . The roads are now in a condition that was not even dreamed of ten years ago, and the good work continues . . . Most of the road this side of the line is in fine shape. For a long time the roads in this county were better than those of our rich neighbor, but we will have to go some to keep up with them now. But then automobiles are not the only conveyances that go over the roads, and the farmers are just as anxious to see a Macadamized road all the way to the county line as anyone else."

A report in the *Oregon Mist* for August 18, 1911, gives the details of road improvement from the Herb Howard farm to the Yankton school, a distance of about one mile. The road bed was prepared twenty-four feet wide with sixteen feet of that rocked to an average depth of ten inches. Clearing the roadway of stumps cost $108, grading cost $1615. The grading down of the hilltop between the church and the cemetery and of the hilltop in front of the Hyde farm involved moving 9000 yards of earth, filling in the valley between the Tarbell and Briggs farms. The grading took nineteen days. Sixteen hundred and twenty yards of rock were applied to the road. This stretch of road was the pride of the neighborhood. It was called a good automobile road.

IV: MINISTERS AND CHURCHES

A holy-minded man of good renown
There was, and poor, a parson of a town . . .
Wide was his parish, with houses far asunder,
Yet he neglected not in rain or thunder,
In sickness or in grief, to pay a call
On the remotest . . .

Chaucer, Prologue (translated)

Jason Lee preached the first sermon in the Northwest at Fort Hall on July 27, 1834, and the first sermon at Vancouver that September. The Methodists set out to carry the Christian message to the scattered people in the wild country. As the Rev. William Roberts saw it, "The people have souls and it is our duty to minister to their spiritual wants."

Lee and his fellow workers held the first camp meeting in the Oregon Territory near what is now Hillsboro beginning on July 13, 1843. Four Methodist ministers were present aside from Lee, but only fourteen people came for the first preaching. On the third day sixty attended and sixteen, including Joe Meek, were moved to profess conversion.

The people at St. Helens built on the bluff overlooking the river a small church building, the third such church building in the Oregon Territory. From 1853 the church was used by circuit-riding ministers, especially those of Methodist, Congregational and Episcopalian charges. The church building was deeded to the Methodists in 1868. At no place in Columbia county were regular and frequent religious services held by any group until into the 1870s.

The Rev. Charles N. Plowman, a young, newly married United Brethren minister, settled on Rock creek in the Nehalem valley in 1876 and held the first religious services in the interior of the county. He organized a Bible class and preached in the area around Vernonia. He worked in the upper Nehalem valley for a decade, exercising his ministerial function in performing marriages for the early settlers. He united John VanBlaricom to Julie Parker on April 1, 1878; Judson Weed to Emaline VanBlaricom, July 13, 1879; Edgar Brand to Hannah VanBlaricom, October 10, 1880; Thomas Tucker to Laura Kerns, September 25, 1881; John Brous to Alice Adams, February 17, 1884; Charles Konkle to Alta Brous, May 9, 1885; Charles Meserve to Louise Congers, June 18, 1887; Newton Parker to Betta Williams, November 5, 1888; Allan Robinson to Adilla Tucker, January 25, 1889. Plowman left the United Brethren conference in 1887 for the Evangelical Association and persuaded this denomination to undertake work in the Nehalem valley.

Plowman bought for $729 a tract of land from Charles Muckle on Milton creek on February 6, 1888, and the Plowman family settled in this new community near the Briggs school while he continued his circuit riding. Plowman and the Rev. C. C. Poling held a week of revival meetings in St. Helens at the end of January 1887. Plowman officiated at the wedding of Herbert A. Corliss and Mrs. Celia E. Gray on October 15, 1887, with F. W. Ridley and Mrs. M. N. Currier as witnesses. The next month, November 23, Plowman united Rudolph Kappler and Sarah Barger in marriage, with Annis and Gordon C. Barger, parents of the young bride, as witnesses. On August 14, 1888, he united Leslie E. Bailey and Winnie B. Emerson in marriage, witnessed by Charles C. and Fred Emerson, brothers of the bride.

Charles Plowman was assigned to preaching missions in Polk county in 1891, regretfully leaving his Columbia county circuits. He wrote affectionate and nostalgic letters back to the county. In his new assignment he had eleven preaching stations, five of which he served twice a month, the other six once a month. In November, 1891, he offered to sell his

Milton creek farm for $1100, "very cheap." But he returned to circuit riding out from Yankton.

He preached at the Yankton school in March 1896, on the subject "What think ye of Christ?" in the evening, after preaching at Bayview schoolhouse in the morning. The Plowmans had ten children, all born after their entry into the Nehalem valley in 1876. In the Yankton school in 1896 were Plowman daughters Ruby, Ethel, Sevilla, and Clara and their cousins, Ruby, Ada, Zorada, Bertha, Walter, Willis and Willie Galloway. In 1898 Plowman was in Hillsboro and sold his Milton creek farm. He served churches in Clackamas county for several years before retiring to a farm near Toledo.

Plowman had an influential place in the religious development of the Nehalem valley. The Evangelicals built the church in Vernonia and in August, 1890, held a camp meeting, the first of what became an annual event of importance to the inner county. The Elmer Everett Nickerson diary kept in the Vernonia years by Mrs. Nickerson, mentions the camp meeting. The Nickersons went to Sunday school the afternoon of June 22, getting home at 5:30. July fourth was marked by speaking, singing, dancing and eating until well past midnight. Saturday, July 19, Mrs. Nickerson "went to the lecture, the first one in Vernonia." On August 17 the Nickersons did not go to Sunday school; but on August 20, Wednesday, the camp meeting commenced. On Sunday Mrs. Nickerson went to the meetings at 11 a.m., 3 p.m. and 8 p.m. and she had "a mob to supper" in the hotel the Nickersons were operating. With meetings all week, Sunday, August 31, was the climax: "Got dinner 1 p.m. went to church 2:30 p.m. and had a lot here to supper. Seven baptized at 3 p.m. went to meeting at 7:30 p.m. the close of camp meeting. Burlingame will preach here every 4th Sunday and Fisher every 2nd Sunday."

The Rev. Martin Burlingame entered Columbia county in 1889. He united Emma Fullerton and Henry Duncan in marriage on June 3, 1889, the earliest of his recorded marriages in the county. He united Letitia Clonnager to

Emmette Stevens in October 21, 1889, and Charles Hart to Annie Bacon on March 27, 1890.

Burlingame, one of the leaders at the Vernonia camp meeting, had a schedule as a circuit-riding minister for the Evangelical Association in 1890, which was indicative of the general assignments of other ministers. He was on the first Sunday of each month in Deer Island at 11 a.m. and at St. Helens at 7:30 p.m. On second Sundays he was at Neer City at 11 a.m., at St. Helens at 7:30 p.m. On Fridays before the third Sundays he was in Clatskanie at 7:30 p.m. and on the third Sundays at Gillton at 11 a.m., Houlton, 2 p.m. On fourth Sundays at Vernonia at 11 a.m. and 7:30 p.m. and at Wilson (presumably a home) at 3 p.m. He was with his family at the second Vernonia camp meeting, August 16-30 in 1891, but by that time his preaching headquarters was at Lafayette.

Mrs. Nickerson's diary gives some sidelights on this second annual August camp meeting. The Burlingame family came from Lafayette for the encampment on Thursday, August 20. On Saturday Mrs. Nickerson went to church but her husband Everett went to a meeting of the Farmers' Alliance. A bear family of three cubs had been an attraction in Vernonia at the Nickerson's all summer. The children of families at the camp flocked around to watch bear antics. Thirteen family tents were up at the camp ground for ten days.

On Sunday, August 23, the Nickersons went to morning camp meeting, had company for dinner and boat-riding in the afternoon, company for supper and then the evening meeting. Mrs. Nickerson, three years married and with a ten-pound baby boy born on May 13, was a busy woman that August. The preachers and their wives all had dinner at the Nickersons on Thursday. The meeting closed Sunday, August 30, with a full day of meetings. In the afternoon John Ward, Julie, Steve and Mrs. Camberling were baptized.

Sunday school Bible study and instruction began in the various communities as schoolhouses or homes were available. At the Briggs school such Sunday school study began in 1887 with the Briggs, Barger and Corliss families taking the lead.

Gordon Cloid Barger was born in Missouri on September 1, 1832, and on January 7, 1855, married Annis Farnsworth, a fourteen-year-old girl. The Bargers soon came to Oregon, living in Portland, Astoria, and again in Portland, where on August 13, 1871, Gordon was ordained into the Methodist ministry, though he was active in the Evangelical Association at Yankton. He did not pursue the ministerial profession except for occasional preaching services, funerals and marriages. He was active in organizing the Briggs school and the Sunday school. He had bought land in the Milton creek watershed in 1883, probably moving his family down from Portland in 1885. Twin sons, Louis and George, were born in Portland in 1873. Gordon C. Barger, or "Old Man" Barger, as he was often called, was a familiar figure in the Yankton area over the years, fishing the streams, walking home with his fishpole over his shoulder and a string of trout in his hand.

A Sunday school was organized in Carico as soon as the schoolhouse was built in 1892. Wilford Miller was the superintendent of the newly formed group. In 1893 he was one of the organizing members of the First Baptist church of Maineville. Apiary organized a Sunday school in 1893. Charles Emerson was the superintendent of the active Sunday school in Houlton.

Revival meetings were held frequently in various localities over the county. Scappoose held a series of poorly attended tent meetings in August, 1891. Scappoose people were too busy with work — or, as some said, with the saloon — to care for their spiritual state. The Rev. Beauchamp held a series of meetings at the Briggs school in December, 1891. He lived in the area and the Beauchamp children, Clarence, Harry and Jessie, were attending the Briggs school.

The Rev. S. E. Faxon from Columbia City preached at Maineville several times through July, August and into the autumn of 1893. He preached in the schoolhouse just before and just after the Baptist church was organized. The Rev. W. N. O'Kelley of the Evangelical Association was a frequent minister at the Maineville church for two or three years. O'Kelley held meetings at the Briggs school in April, 1894, and a series of meetings was held there in September, 1895, and also in January and in April 1896. The Rev. Charles N. Plowman, recently returned from Polk county, held the January meetings and reported sixteen converts. His Evangelical converts did not add to the membership of the newly organized First Baptist church of Maineville, where the membership remained a stable dozen for a decade. In April 1896, the Rev. Gilman Parker held a week of meetings under the leadership of the Baptist church. He stayed at the home of Deacon Charles Tarbell, who wrote that Parker was "a fine speaker and a very devoted man." Again, in January 1897, protracted meetings — as these revivalist sessions were often called — were held at the Yankton school and "progressed nicely" as a reporter noted, with "a large number preparing to be saved and washed in the waters of Milton Creek."

A revivalist preacher in Warren so aroused the ire of the local correspondent for the *Oregon Mist* that the correspondent leveled a six-inch column of advice at the preacher, telling him that the community was made up of good honest citizens and not "sinners" who needed to be scolded like children. He advised the revivalist to change his approach if he really wanted to make any converts.

The first marriage recorded in the county was performed by John Hawkins, J. P., at Rainier, uniting Francis M. Phelan and Catherine Spencer, March 26, 1855. The earliest marriage solemnized by a minister was recorded June 1, 1855. The Rev. Tom Hendrickson united Daniel Boon Armstrong and Elizabeth Bouser.

Most of the marriages in the county in the early decades were performed by secular officials, such as Dean Blanchard, county judge in Rainier. James McBride, a minister, married Thomas A. McBride to Mary Merrill, February 7, 1875. Martin Judy, John Flinn, Sidney Wood, James Sellwood, James Matthews, A. Lauback, S. D. Earl, S.L. Lee are all recorded as officiating at weddings during the 1870s and 1880s. E. S. Bryant, a minister in the

Christadelphian church — as he signed himself — officiated for three weddings.

A search of the marriages recorded during the 1890s in Columbia county shows that more than fifty Protestant ministers were active in the county during that decade. The record shows only one marriage with a Roman Catholic priest officiating. The Methodists were the most numerous of the identifiable affiliations, with the Evangelical Association next. Many of the performing ministers gave no indication of the church in which they held ordination.

The Methodists had churches at St. Helens, Rainier, Clatskanie, Houlton and Warren, and other preaching stations with ministers often assigned for only a year or even a briefer period, always serving several churches and preaching stations. Although Methodist preaching began in the county as early as 1852 at St. Helens, with a community church built in 1853, and 1854 at Rainier, with ministers assigned to cover those stations by those dates, the assignment of Methodist ministers to the county was irregular for decades. Rainier, after a few preaching ventures in the 1850s had no regular minister assigned, according to conference records, until 1895 when it as a parish was yoked to St. Helens. St. Helens was served in 1884 by Thomas Brown, in 1885-6 by S. L. Lee, in 1887-8 by C. Alderson and 1889 by A.H. Nichols. Clatskanie has no recorded Methodist minister before 1890.

Throughout the 1890s the Methodist conference made regular assignments of ministers to St. Helens, Rainier, Clatskanie. The ministers assigned also served at other preaching stations in the county: Deer Island, Reuben, Yankton, Valley, Peris, Apiary, Delena, Stehman and others. In 1895-97 the same minister served St. Helens and Rainier; in 1890-91 the St. Helens church and Clatskanie were yoked. Each minister must have covered three or four preaching stations at least once a month. The following Methodist ministers had assignments in the county during the 1890s: A. G. Child, Henry C. Child, W. M. McCart, F. L. Moore, O. A. White, Martin Judy, W. L. Blackwell, H. T. Atkinson, D. M. Shannon, J. M. Smith, E. V. Smith, George

Grovenor Haley, Donald McLachlin, A. C. Fairchild, Martin Burlingame.

A new Methodist church was dedicated in Houlton May 14, 1898, with the Rev. Haley preaching the dedicatory sermon. The St. Helens Methodist church built on the bluff burned in 1899. The church bought a lot in the center of town at St. Helens and Columbia streets and on December 17, 1900, dedicated the new building, which cost $1400. This building stood opposite the city hall, serving the community for over twenty years there. Bishop Earl Cranston preached the dedication sermon and in the afternoon gave a lecture on China, where he had served as a missionary. Warren dedicated a Methodist church in May 1901. In March 1901 Mr. Ford, the St. Helens photographer, gave a benefit magic lantern show at the Methodist church featuring pictures of a recent trip he had taken. The Free Methodist church in Houlton was dedicated in April 1907.

In 1850 there were 393 members of established Methodist churches in Oregon, and that number was near 3% of the population. Methodists increased in numbers along with population increase. In 1860 thirty-nine churches in Oregon had 1336 members, about 2.5% of the population. The next decade was more productive: the 2867 Methodists were 3.1% of the population. In 1880 the ratio dropped to 1.1% — the lowest ratio recorded. The next decade Methodists increased in number in Oregon from 2,980 to 6,482, slightly more than 2% of the population. In 1900 the ratio was 2.5%; 1910, 2.7%; 1920, 2.6%; 1930, 3.21%; 1940, 3.3%; 1950, 2.8%. Thus over its first active century, Oregon Methodism held generally stable with population growth.

The 1886 Oregon Methodist Episcopal Conference report lists only the St. Helens church in Columbia county; but the 1894 report lists churches at Clatskanie with 42 members and St. Helens with 12 members. In 1900 Columbia county had 105 Methodist church members in the three churches: Clatskanie, 60 members; Rainier, 25; St. Helens, 20. In 1910 the church at Houlton was also included and the four churches had 174 members: Clatskanie, 85; Houlton, 31; Rainier, 36; St. Helens, 22. In the next decade the membership in the county doubled, even though the church at Houlton was lost through consolidation with St. Helens. Clatskanie in 1920 had 158 members; Rainier, 45; St. Helens, 152.

Thus the ratio of Methodists to the total population in the county was not keeping up with the ratio in the state. Methodist membership in the county was less than 1% in the 1890s, about 1½% in 1910 and about 2½% in 1920.

The Rev. Martin Burlingame was assigned to the Rainier Methodist church in 1898. He had before that time been active in the Evangelical Association for a decade. He bought from the Evangelical Association in St. Helens lot eleven in block eighteen for one hundred dollars on November 2, 1889. Charles S. Emerson and Gordon C. Barger acted on behalf of the Evangelical Association in the property sale.

In the winter of 1891-92 Rev. Burlingame sparked the building of Providence Chapel, an Evangelical church, at Houlton. It was begun on December 14 and was dedicated March 18, 1892, "Completed by the energetic labors of Rev. M. Burlingame" and N. A. Perry, B. W. Plummer, L. Meeker, George Kelley, Charles S. Emerson, the Muckle brothers, Captain A. Henderson, H. L. Howard, W. L. Sterm, A. P. Clark, Fred Emerson, Charles Simmons, J. Urie, A. E. Emerson, and J. Emmerands, all of whom contributed money, labor or both. The land on which the church stood was donated by Mr. and Mrs. Henshaw. A delegation of folk from up Milton creek — Yankeetown then — came in over the muddy wagon road for the dedication service. Charles S. Emerson was superintendent of the Sunday school.

Burlingame was much in demand for marriages in the county in the first years of the decade. Then for five years he left the county going to Lafayette. He returned to serve the Evangelical churches in Houlton, Goble, Bay View and St. Helens in 1897. He and his family are listed as members of the St. Helens Methodist church in 1898, when he was appointed minister to the Rainier church. His daughter May began teaching school at the age of sixteen in Bachelor Flat;

teaching also in Multnomah county, and in Peris, where she was also superintendent of the newly organized Sunday school. She was in December, 1899, married to Fred Briggs and began her years as a Yankton resident.

Martin Burlingame held revival meetings in Scappoose between Christmas and New Year's, 1897, and again in March. In January he held two weeks of services in Houlton.

He took charge of the Scappoose parish of the Methodist church in the summer of 1898 and sparked and masterminded the building of the church, doing much of the construction himself. The building was dedicated free of debt in mid-August, Dr. William Holman Iliff from Portland presiding. Burlingame went to Rainier as the Methodist pastor for a year, his only Methodist appointment. He next lived in Deer Island, then at Woodlawn in Portland in 1902, where his wife cared for their grandson, Martin Briggs, for a few weeks while May Briggs, the mother, operated the Oriental Hotel in St. Helens.

In addition to the Rev. Martin Burlingame in the Evangelical Association were Gordon C. Barger, W. N. O'Kelley, James A. Ray, F.W. Launer, Gilbert McElroy and Charles N. Plowman. The United Brethren was represented by the Rev. W. H. Palmer, R. A. Slyter and Phys Gwynn.

The Nehalem valley had a Swedish church for several years, dating from 1881, its eight members being visited occasionally by the Rev. August Westerberg of Portland. C. Priecing performed a wedding representing the German M. E. church. The Rev. George A. John served a German Methodist group in Scappoose for a time about 1897. The Rev. John H. Lumijarvi of the Apostolic Lutheran church in Clatsop and Columbia counties united Jacob Tolva and Greta Madhilta Krym in marriage on February 12, 1897, witnessed by Oscar Waisanen and John Wiemela.

A Roman Catholic missionary priest, the Rev. Dr. Hubert Fisher, from Astoria, performed a wedding for the Polish St. Joseph Roman Catholic church near Valley, on September 11, 1894. Joe Deleski vouched for Francis Sakawicz and Anton Redzewski for a marriage license. Witnesses were Anton Kierowski and Antonio Rambolski. A social evening and dance followed the wedding at the Joseph White home. The Roman Catholic community was dominantly Polish but some of the settlers were French or German.

Mr. and Mrs. Valentine Gliniecki on December 2, 1891, deeded to the Roman Catholic Archbishop John Seghers and his successors for one dollar, a piece of land expressly "for the use and benefit of the St. Joseph Poland Catholic church and for school and cemetery purposes." The *Oregon Mist* for March 24, 1893, reported, "The new church out in the Poland section of Bunker Hill is completed." The sum of $274.25 had been raised, but the cost of the building was $355.66, leaving an indebtedness owing to Mr. Valentine Gliniecki of $61.41. When Mrs. Catherine Karth died on July 22, 1895, she was buried in the St. Joseph cemetery.

Roman Catholic church activity developed slowly in the county. Aside from the St. Joseph church in the Nehalem valley — which was served as a mission station from Astoria while the church stood — Catholic evidence in the county is scarce until well into the twentieth century. When the triple drowning hit the Sobieski family in the Tedford creek dam July 4, 1894, a priest was brought down from Portland to consecrate graves in the Yankton cemetery beside the Baptist church.

Roman Catholic services began in Rainier and St. Helens sometime before 1910. In October, 1912, the *Oregon Mist* noted that the Rev. Father Bronagel, who had been in charge of the Rainier and St. Helens Catholic churches "for several years," was moving to South Dakota, to be replaced by the Rev. Father Fisher. Rainier dedicated the Catholic church there on May 15, 1910. The St. Helens Catholic church was dedicated in August, 1911. Scappoose had dedicated a small chapel in June, 1911. Clatskanie dedicated a chapel in 1917, which was served from Astoria.

Although the Baptists had over a hundred and fifty churches in Oregon, that denomination was represented in Columbia county only by the First Baptist church of Maineville, the church sponsored by Deacon Charles Tarbell, organized August 12, 1893. It had only a dozen charter members, seven of them Tarbells, and at the close of the century it had added no new members. It had no regular minister assigned to it for years. The church, even with a good building built in 1903 by Deacon Tarbell, did not thrive. During his last — his eighty-fourth — year, Charles Tarbell wrote of the church which was so close to his heart:

"We are having a variety of preaching this summer. The first Sunday in the month have a Holiness man . . . . We rather enjoy his sermons. The second Sunday a Medthodist (Charles never could spell Methodist!) that no one likes so he gets quite a small hearing. The third Sunday a little Baptist that preaches fairly good sermons but is a Southerner and goes in for gymnasticks and a ff voice so you can imagine how it sets on the ears of a staid old man . . . Sunday, p.m. Been to church and listened to a sermon by our little gymnasium preacher."

In November of that year, 1913, "They have sent us a minister that is a fine preacher . . ." Charles was better satisfied. On the following April, Rev. Leonard W. Riley, the president of McMinnville College, came to deliver a funeral sermon over the body of Charles Lucius Tarbell, as he had four years earlier for Nancy Tarbell. The remains of both are across the road from the church which they had built.

The Anglican church was the second religious body to have a representative in the Oregon country when the Rev. Herbert Beaver and his wife Jane arrived at Fort Vancouver from England in September, 1836. Beaver was active as a minister in the Vancouver area for two years before he returned again to England.

The Rev. Wm. Richmond of the Episcopal church came to Oregon as a missionary in 1851, holding his first service in Portland on May 18, 1851, in the Methodist church. In 1852 he visited Milton at the mouth of Milton creek and made plans for future worship there. The Rev. John McCarty succeeded him in 1853 and McCarty performed the first Episcopal service in St. Helens in the new church on the bluff. He wrote of St. Helens as a very small village and said, "I could not find any Episcopalian in the place. As St. Helens is likely to become a place of some importance I intend to visit St. Helens and Milton occasionally."

The Charles Tarbell home at Yankton about 1905. From the left: Alice Brown, Iva Tarbell, Charles and Nancy Tarbell, Lawrence Tarbell holding Enid Tarbell, Emma Tarbell, Beth Brown.

When the Muckle families came to Columbia county the Episcopalian prospect improved. The Jacob George family came for Jacob to work in the Muckle mill. Episcopal services were held in St. Helens at intervals over the years by priests from Portland. In March, 1897, a lot was secured, funds were solicited and Christ Episcopal church was dedicated in May. Ten clergymen from Portland came to participate in the ceremonies, with Bishop Morris presiding.

The Rev. William A. Muhlenberg Breck was appointed vicar to Christ Episcopal church in 1901 and served the church twenty years. The attractive small church building on the plaza in front of the county court house has long been a landmark in St. Helens.

The American Board of Commissioners for Foreign Missions sent Dr. Marcus Whitman and his party to the Oregon country in 1836, continuing the missionary work which the New England Congregationalists had earlier begun in Hawaii and the South Pacific. In 1847 Dr. and Mrs. Whitman were massacred near present Walla Walla, Washington, but members of that mission and others continued their work in the Willamette valley and especially in the Tualatin valley.

The first Congregational church in the Oregon country was organized in 1837 or 1838. By 1850 five churches were organized, having a total membership of twenty-five. In 1860 ten churches had a total membership of 225. In 1870 nine churches had 450 members. In 1880 twelve churches had 785 members. Between 1880 and 1890 twenty-four churches were organized and the total Congregational membership was two thousand. In 1891 eleven new Congregational churches were started in the one year. But not all of these churches thrived — or even survived.

Thomas Condon, the pioneer geologist of Oregon country, began his career as a missionary under the Congregational churches. He went to St. Helens in 1853 directly from his trip around the Horn on a clipper ship. He built a home on the high bluff and held preaching services in the town church also on the bluff. Condon also organized a village school. He was in 1854 pastor of the Congregational church in Forest

Grove; in 1857 pastor of the Congregational church in Albany; in 1862 second pastor of the Congregational church in The Dalles. He went to Pacific University in Forest Grove to teach in 1873, and began his work at the University of Oregon in 1876. Thomas Condon was a significant pioneer minister who did a great work as pioneer teacher and writer on the geology of the Northwest.

The down river county had long looked toward Portland for leadership, especially after the Lewis and Clark Exposition in 1905. The White Temple of the Baptist church, the Taylor Street Methodist church and the First Congregational church of Portland all exerted an influence on the area around. Congregationalist ministers came into Columbia county from Portland as well as from Forest Grove and across the Columbia river. Cowlitz river and the Cathlamet had Congregational churches. Various circuit riding ministers held preaching services in the county.

Scappoose started a Congregational church as an organization in 1888 under the care of the Rev. J. G. Gordon. It was formally established in May, 1890, organizing members including Mrs. J. G. Watts, L. B. Shoemaker, L. P. Whitney, Mrs. P. B. Stevens, Mrs. Adam Stump, Mrs. Asa Holaday. Its incorporation papers were dated May 31, 1891.

John James Staub was at Scappoose as a summer student minister in 1891 while he was at Pacific Theological Seminary in Berkely. After graduation Staub went to Scappoose for a year as the regular minister of the church. Scappoose at the beginning of the 1890s had about forty families within the community. The Sunday school had fifty persons on its rolls. Under Staub's ministry the Scappoose church built a building and added 21 names to the church membership roll.

In 1891 the Rev. W. C. Wise was preaching at Rainier, but he also had six preaching stations aside from Rainier.

The Rev. A. H. Bauman held preaching services at Rainier in parts of 1891-92 and Staub also preached in Rainier twice a month. The two men held two weeks of meetings in the summer. But ministers found that promoting Christian doctrine and work was difficult in this unsettled county. Over and over again the ministers reported on "the indifference of the many and the unsettled and roving disposition of others. They are here today and gone tomorrow. The omnipresent saloon is here, running night and day and every day in the week." In both Rainier and Scappoose the saloon element was strong.

The Rev. John J. Staub left Columbia county for a long career as minister to the Sunnyside Congregational church in Portland, which later changed its name to the Staub Memorial Church.

Scappoose was without a pastor for a time. The Rev. George Baker took over the charges of Rainier and Scappoose for a few months in 1893, but he reported that the "Germans all went over to the Methodists," where John Wesley Beckley, a Portland resident, was preaching, leaving the Scappoose Congregational church with only six members, all women. What had four years earlier looked like a promising Congregational church for the community was disheartened and defeated.

Baker served the Scappoose church for a few months in 1894, but resigned for health reasons. In 1894, in spite of the hard times, the ladies of Rainier put on a money-raising event toward building a Congregational church in that city. They raised $40.

The Rev. Charles E. Philbrook came from Kansas to St. Helens to visit his sister in June, 1895. He found an ailing brother-in-law, making it desirable for him to remain near his sister and her family. He preached in the Scappoose church, at Warren, Houlton and Yankton.

Philbrook was a mature minister. His sister Sarah, Mrs. Lamont, was born in Bath, Maine, in 1831. He was born there on May 8, 1841. He spent some years in seeing America before deciding on his profession. He left Maine for California in 1859, visited his widowed sister at St. Helens in 1863. In 1868 he decided to enter the ministry, went to school, was ordained and married Teresa Watson, born in 1845, in 1872. He served Congregational churches in California and Kansas before returning to St. Helens for his second visit with his sister Sarah.

When Philbrook went to the Scappoose church it had six disheartened woman members. In eighteen months he improved the situation to seventeen women, four men members. But his most important work was away from Scappoose. In September, 1895, he was asked to preach in St. Helens on a regular basis twice a month. The editor of the *Oregon Mist* spoke favorably of his preaching. His St. Helens followers decided in 1896 to organize a Congregational church, with three men and eighteen women as charter members. Most of these twenty-one were adult heads of families. The work of Philbrook in Scappoose, St. Helens, Houlton, Yankton was impressive. One comment read, "This is the greatest religious movement St. Helens has ever known." In 1899 he gave up the Scappoose church to the Rev. Richard M. Jones, who preached at Scappoose and Rainier. Jones found both of these charges tough going. His services were not well attended. "The lodge and the dance are more popular than the church," he found, and he said in both towns the saloons were doing great harm.

Philbrook served four preaching stations aside from his St. Helens charge, one being Bachelor Flat. In that preaching station five persons organized a church in 1899, but it did not last. Philbrook was a personable man, well-liked for his direct practicality. One of his first projects in Columbia county was to lead his Scappoose congregation to raise money to buy a cow for a destitute family. The Yankton correspondent wrote favorably of his ministry. He was called upon widely for wedding and funeral services.

Even the staunchly Evangelical Emerson family called upon Philbrook to conduct the funeral services for Mrs. Charles E. Emerson (nee Almira Hooper). When James Braddock of Houlton was killed by a falling tree on the Thomas Holstein place, the Rev. Philbrook was called upon for the funeral service.

When the time came in 1902 for him to answer a call to the church at Silvan, Washington, St. Helens said, "We have bid goodbye to our much-loved Brother Philbrook and wife."

The Rev. Philbrook's son George achieved national distinction. He attended Whitman College, then Notre Dame

University, where he was a star tackle and a discus champion. He was also a successful competitor in the 1912 Olympics in Stockholm.

Philbrook, while minister to the church on Lummi Island in Washington, performed the wedding of his son George and Miss Roxie Ferryman of Indiana at the St. Helens Congregational church in July, 1914. The Rev. Philbrook died the following year.

The Rev. Philbrook's other son, Watson, taught in the Houlton school and in Columbia county before going to the Phillipine Islands to teach.

Columbia county's Congregational churches ran into hard times after Philbrook left the county. Richard Jones at Rainier and Scappoose never felt quite equal to the task. In 1903 the Rev. G. A. Taggart had the Rainier and St. Helens churches, being at St. Helens twice a month. In 1906 the Rev. Neil Carmichael was at Rainier and St. Helens with not very effective results. Scappoose under the Rev. William L. Upshaw in 1909 seemed to be looking up again, but at the end of the decade the St. Helens and Rainier churches were without pastors and were discouraged. It was not until 1913 that these two churches seemed to revive again, St. Helens under the Rev. Frank Meyer and Rainier under the Rev. David Joplin.

The late Edson Clapp of Portland, son of the Rev. Cephas F. Clapp, who was the missionary superintendent of the Congregational conference for many years, remembered going with his father about 1910 in one of the early vintage automobiles to the Scappoose church where his father preached and he played the violin at the service. Edson said that his father was an effective speaker who always had a large fund of anecdotes and illustrations to use in making his points.

Infidelity and indifference, the dance and the saloon, the call of the out-of-doors and the river were continuously obstructing the efforts of the many earnest ministers representing many different branches of Christian faith to bring the people into wholesome and productive lives. The struggles to establish churches on firm foundation wore out many men who started their tasks in a spirit of hope and expectation.

In 1895 in Oregon twenty-seven Congregational ministers were trying to cover forty-three churches and seventeen out-stations and sixty Sunday schools. And what was the lot of their wives? Plenty of hard work with small pay. Often they had large families and little to do with. Moving frequently from town to town, these wives could be thankful that here and there a missionary box or barrel, like an angel of mercy, dropped in on them from some eastern missionary group to relieve their needs and gladden their hearts.

The Rev. George C. Hall from the Astoria Congregational church expressed on June 25, 1889, a feeling which must have been that of many a Columbia county minister over the next twenty-five years. "July is not a good month in which to make a report of the spiritual condition of churches near a great seaside resort: what with steamerloads of people coming down here on excursions every Sunday, with the blare of brass bands on the streets, with the city full of pleasure seekers, with picnic excursions going hither and thither, with our own people scattered here and there — the tendencies are very demoralizing. It is extremely difficult to maintain a truly spiritual condition under such disheartening circumstances . . . [people] prefer a boat ride on Sunday to an hour of worship.''

The population of Columbia county was fluctuating and mobile, depending largely on timber harvest and wood products. Men were either single or away from their families. Women were burdened with endless household tasks. Even though the development of the Oregon country was spearheaded by religious motivation and earnest leaders, churches did not flourish in the Northwest. Church membership throughout the century and a half of Northwest settlement has been low, in fact the lowest in any part of the United States. The percentage of population holding church membership has been consistently low in Oregon, and the percentage in Columbia county must have been for the fifty years after 1870 lower even than that of the state as a whole.

It is not that there was any philosophical or theological opposition to the Christian religion. The county had few if any village atheists or agnostics. The great debate between science and religion following in the wake of Darwin and Huxley did not leave any evidence in the county. Even the widely heard agnostic Robert Ingersoll, who spoke several times in Oregon, made no impression on Columbia county. It may be that the churches and the ministers did not speak with sufficient directness to the needs of the people to overcome their indifference, the appeal of the social saloon, the lure of a boat on the river, the ever-present call of the woods and the streams.

Such ministers as Burlingame and Philbrook achieved results from their labors, even though sometimes the results seemed illusory. In 1910 the young unmarried Aaron Allen Heist was appointed to the St. Helens Methodist church, coming from a ministry at Warrenton. He had not yet been to seminary. The St. Helens Methodist church was strategically located directly facing the new St. Helens city hall and near the county court house. Heist in the spring of 1911 was in a Portland hospital for two months with typhoid fever, requiring months of convalescing. When he went to St. Helens the church was a small struggling congregation of some twenty people. When he left St. Helens at the end of two years he left a congregation of over eighty active members.

The official records of the Methodist conference reveal this significant growth. When S. L. Lee was minister in 1886 the congregation consisted of sixty persons, twenty-five of them over 15 years of age. In 1900 membership was 20, with about 40 in the Sunday school. This was an increase from 12 members in 1894, when 35 were in the Sunday school. In 1910 Heist came as minister in the fall, with the Rev. Asa Sleeth reporting that the St. Helens church had 22 members. In 1920 membership was 152. Financial support for the total church program increased from $681 in 1910 to $1908 in 1920.

Heist was a handsome well-built small man with a classic Greek profile. He was intelligent, alert, hardworking and ambitious. His sermon topic on February 11, 1912, was "Abraham Lincoln, the Christian." He spoke in a quiet manner but with force and conviction. His sermons were carefully prepared. He respected his calling and was a fulltime working minister. The Rev. Asa Sleeth who had preceded him in the St. Helens church received a salary of $120. Heist earned his thousand dollar salary.

The official board of the church in 1910 included some of the St. Helens community leaders: Wm. Ross, Dr. L. G. Ross, Aden Ross, Dr. Edwin A. Ross, Mrs. William Ross, Martin White, L. R. Rutherford, Mrs. H. E. LaBarre, Mrs. C. H. Thompson, Miss Elsie Phillips, E. E. Quick, Mrs. C. M. Gray, C. M. Gray. Heist organized the Sunday school and an active young people's group and an active Ladies Aid Society. A building committee was organized to plan remodeling and enlarging the church building.

Heist was a popular and successful minister. He left the St. Helens church in September, 1912, to enter Northwestern University Theological Seminary. When he finished his theological work at Northwestern he was appointed pastor of the Rose City Park Methodist church in Portland. He returned to St. Helens to marry Miss Elsie Phillips in the St. Helens church in June, 1917. In May, 1918, their son was born.

In October of that year Heist was moved to the Astoria Methodist church where he served until 1921, when he moved to Aberdeen, Washington. He resigned his pastoral duties in April, 1923, to become field secretary for the Methodist Federation of Social Service, with headquarters in Chicago. His sister Laura and another sister were life long missionaries to India.

Heist left a going Methodist church in St. Helens. He was succeeded as pastor by the Rev. E. L. Luther, then by the Rev. F. N. Sandifer and by the Rev. Albert H. Hisey, a kind and noble-hearted man who served during the World War I years and until the summer of 1920.

V: SCHOOLS AND TEACHERS

*Everything is useful which contributes to fix in the
principles and practices of virtue.*

Thomas Jefferson

An entertainment and social gathering of the community
took place in a new school building five miles up Milton
creek from St. Helens on the stormy January twenty-sixth
evening of 1887. It was a celebration and a money-raising
venture. Through the rainy evening over primitive wagon
trails the few scattered settlers assembled to mark an
important beginning of what was to be a community. They
had organized a school and built a school building.

On August 2, 1886, James Muckle, Jr., and his wife,
deeded one acre of land to school district No. 30 for five
dollars, the land, ten by sixteen rods, to be used as a school
grounds forever, or to revert to the Muckle heirs. The Rev.
Gordon Cloid Barger was chairman and Laura Howard
Briggs (Mrs. Charles H. Briggs) was the clerk of the board.
Money had been solicited for the building of the
schoolhouse, and the entertainment in the new building was
to clear its last small debt. The meeting raised twenty-three
dollars and sixty-five cents.

S. L. Lee, young minister of the St. Helens Methodist
church, attended the gathering, enjoying the luxurious
supper served amid the usual backwoods bustle and festive
fellowship. Lee delivered the appropriate extended prayer of
Thanksgiving. Eight natives of Sweden, from the Nehalem
valley, sang a hymn in their native language. Miss Elizabeth
Jones gave a commendable reading of "Rebecca at the
Well." The school and the community were at a
commencement.

The well-built frame one-room school was from its opening a focal point for the few families living within reach. A Sunday school was organized for meetings there and itinerant preachers used it for preaching services. Even politicians seeking votes were sometimes able to fill it. This building in 1887 was the most substantial schoolhouse in the interior of the county.

The Vernonia area was first settled in 1874. Israel Putnam Spencer, recently arrived in Vernonia from Michigan, wrote on November 7, 1876, "We are going to commence work on the schoolhouse here tomorrow." The building thus built by volunteer labor was of hewn logs erected on the claim of Clark L. Parker. This early structure was replaced in 1891. A notice appearing in the *Oregon Mist* that Vernonia was building a church and a school elicited a response from a Clatskanie reporter: "A new schoolhouse and a church are the things that Clatskanie wants and it seems a little strange that their neighboring town in the woods is going to get ahead with both buildings." Clatskanie built both church and school within the year, and Rainier, too, built a new and larger schoolhouse in 1891. Houlton built a suitable school in 1889, replacing an earlier one at Milton. School began in the new Houlton building on February 11 with thirty-two pupils representing eleven families.

The county school boundary book in the St. Helens school office does not give beginning dates for many of the school districts, but the district numbers give a generally dependable order in which schools started in the county, though some were started informally before a number was granted.

At the end of the 1880s and early in the 1890s school districts mushroomed over the inner county. Every little settlement wanted its school and it didn't take many farm families to comprise a settlement. Sunnyside school at Fishhawk was number 8, Beaver Home east of Scappoose was 9, Marshland west of Clatskanie was 10. Columbia City, Fern Hill at Vernonia, Rainier, Pleasant Hill at Vernonia, Hazel Grove at Clatskanie, Stehman out from Rainier came in sequence. Mrs. Lucy Stehman Howard came from the

Stehman family. Ollie Rice, who married Guy Tarbell of Yankton, was a pupil in October, 1891, in the Stehman school. She taught the Yankton school two years before her marriage in 1902.

Pittsburg was on the wagon trail cleared out through the wilderness from the Nehalem valley over Bunker Hill in 1879. The Peter Brous family settled on a claim on the river in 1877. A log cabin schoolhouse was built in 1879, a frame school in 1884. Pittsburg became county school number 17. Pleasant Vale at Mist was organized as number 18 but it did not long survive.

Rock Hill, Goble, Chapman, Natal, Mayger, Oak Ranch not far from Natal, Quincy, Alder Grove, Rock Creek, South Scappoose and Downing all were established about 1884. Number 29, Downing, is dated 1886 and Yankton, number 30, was organized in 1886.

Bachelor Flat and Kist, numbers 54 and 55, were about the last school districts to organize in the county. Columbia Heights school, between Houlton and Yankton, using an abandoned number, was organized in 1914 and endured for a few scant years. It was the school where the author received his eighth grade graduation certificate, signed by his mother as school clerk. The school was taught by one of the Miller twins.

The only academy in the county before the twentieth century was established in Columbia City by Joseph Caples. Caples dreamed dreams and made plans for a major city on the river, platting the town in 1871. The tuition academy opened in 1872 on block 26, Second street, with Major E. G. Adams from Yale College as teacher. Tuition was five dollars for twelve weeks. At its maximum development the academy had two teachers and sixty pupils, but the visions of a growing city evaporated and the academy faded away.

Mrs. Flora Calhoun attempted a private tuition school in St. Helens in February, 1887, but it failed to develop.

The Carico school, number 34, met in a private home in November, 1888. A schoolhouse was built for school and church use in 1891. Eleven pupils were enrolled in the summer of 1893. The Peris community organized as school

70

The Cedar Grove school No. 44, about 1901. Stumps in the yard, trees nearby, a riding horse waiting for one of the pupils. Identifications by J.R. Holmes, whose family were early settlers in the Delena area. Front row: Harry Palm?, Raymond Jones, Warren Young, Melville Young. Second Row: Olaf Soderstrom, Ellen Lindahl, Nora Lindahl, Mable Jones, Velma Young, Claud Holmes, Clyde Holmes, ??, Oscar Lindberg, Omer Holmes, ??, Johnny Holmes, Adolph Lindberg?. Back Row: Arthur Young (teacher), Florey Young, Emily Lindberg, Setina Palm, Ellen Shelberg, Jenny Lindberg.

district number 43 on June 20, 1891. B. F. Pope completed a log building on the farm of C. L. Ayres and school began on June 21, 1892, with Richard H. Bailey as teacher. Bailey finished the Peris summer term and then taught the winter term in the Briggs school. Miss Adelle Pugh was teaching the winter term in the Peris school when she and her eleven pupils enjoyed the excitement of being visited by a large black bear. Miss Caples of the Columbia City family taught at Peris in the spring of 1894. That winter Cornelius C. Moyer taught the children in his own home. Richard Bailey taught the summer term with 15 pupils.

The Deer Island schoolhouse was built in the summer of 1893.

Miss Benser finished a three months term of school at Valley in June, 1892, before a schoolhouse was available.

In June, 1893, Ole Erickson deeded one acre of land in section 31, 7 N, 3 W to the new school district #41, the Valley district, for one dollar. Valley developed into a self-conscious community with an active correspondent to the *Oregon Mist*, a new post office in June, 1895, school district boundary set in June, 1895, and a new schoolhouse in 1896. Miss Tillie Cheldelin, from a Vernonia family, the teacher in June, 1896, reported nine boys and ten girls enrolled in the school, with an average attendance of seventeen. Students having perfect attendance records were Rose and Leontine Dupont, Martha and John Sintek, Katie and Mattie Dalatski, Sofa and Conrad Ramblaski. Miss Cheldelin also taught the three months summer term.

Iris W. Tarbell came to the Milton creek settlement from Maine with her family in the summer of 1892 when she was fourteen years old, a tall, nearsighted girl much given to reading and reciting poems which she easily memorized. She took some extra work in the Briggs school with the young teacher Ernest S. Faxon, took the county examination to become a certified teacher in February, 1896, and again in May, apparently failing to pass all the subjects on the first try when 25 of the 44 candidates received certificates. She attended the teachers' institute in July, but apparently did not get a school until the April term at Valley, 1897. The times were difficult and teachers' average salary had been reduced to $35 for men and $32.57 per month for women. Iris Tarbell had 12 students enrolled in the Valley school, with an average attendance of nine the first month. Rene and Leontine Dupont and Eva and John Sobieski had good attendance records. In May the average attendance dropped to eight, but the teacher reported that "general deportment and interest were good." Martha and Ludwick Sintek had their names listed for good attendance.

Iris Tarbell was a romantically idealistic teacher with a Baptist bent to her evangelistic Christianity. Her grandfather was Deacon Charles Tarbell and she was a charter member of the First Baptist church of Maineville. She saw her teaching profession as a call to influence her pupils in more that intellectual pursuits. While teaching that first backwoods school of a dozen youngsters she wrote a poem which expressed her hope for the fruits of her work. It appeared in the *Oregon Mist* June 11, 1897.

THE TEACHER'S SOWING

I think as I face the children,
How grand is the task that is mine!
To train the minds of girls and boys
That they may in future shine.

. . . .

Our ways and acts they are watching,
And they listen to what we say:
Like the "bread cast on the waters,"
They will return to us some day.

. . . .

The young Iris Tarbell, age about fourteen, before she left Maine for Columbia county.

The Rev. Thomas Condon taught pupils in a school building on the bluff in St. Helens in 1853, but it was not until February, 1881, that land was deeded to the St. Helens district for a school building, which was ready for the fall term. Emerson E. Quick, born in Indiana in 1852, graduate of Pacific University in 1877, taught the school before he was elected county clerk. He also was an early teacher in the Briggs school.

Gillton, to be named Warren in 1895, had school number 7. Its post office was established in 1890. C. H. Jones, a graduate of the normal school at Monmouth, taught the spring term of school in 1891 at Gillton before going to St.

Helens to teach the fall term. His fall term there closed November 25, having had 53 pupils enrolled, with an average attendance of 44½. Jones began a remarkable rise to prominence with that year of teaching in Gillton and St. Helens. In the fall of 1894 he was principal of the Oswego school; in the fall of 1895 of the McMinnville school; and in the fall of 1896 of the Salem school, with twelve teachers.

He married Miss Blanche Miller of St. Helens, also a teacher, in June, 1895, keeping his ties and friendships in Columbia county. He studied law and returned to St. Helens to practice.

The county school superintendent, J. G. Watts, began administering examinations for teachers and recording certificates in 1889. Watts was an energetic promoter of country school education, working to improve the quality of teaching. He arranged for the first teachers' institute in the county in Clatskanie the first week in August, 1891. The twenty-five teachers attending met in a hotel which furnished them a place to sleep and meals for the week for three dollars each.

Watts prepared a report of the educational resources of the county on March 17, 1892. There were 1885 persons of legal school age out of a total population of 5191. This was an increase from the 1770 school age pupils of the year before. The 51 organized district schools in the county, with 38 schoolhouses, had an enrollment of 1086 pupils, an increase from 908 the year before. The average length of the school year was 4 4/5 months. The male teachers averaged $45.25 a month for the actual period of teaching; the average female teacher received $38.50 a month. Watts reported that 21 of the 38 schoolhouses contained Webster's dictionaries, probably the total library of most of them. Watts concluded his report: "Columbia county shows a splendid advance in educational facilities." Watts had well earned his fifteen dollars a month salary over his years as superintendent.

The *Oregon Mist* for January 28, 1887, stated: "Parties having business with the county superintendent of schools will find him in his office the last Saturday of each month."

The temper of public support of the government may be estimated from a comment by the editor: "The proposition to raise the salaries of the county judge and treasurer should be defeated. Our taxes are high enough. The treasurer at present gets $200 a year and the actual work of his office can be done in ten days." The county judge received $300 a year. Though there was active expansion of the county schools during these years there was little inclination to increase monetary support.

T. J. Cleeton was elected county school superintendent in 1892 to start what was to be a long career in Columbia county. He was teacher at Clatskanie, then at Rainier. He studied law, was admitted to the bar and successfully ran for the legislature. As a candidate for public office he was much discussed and reported on in the *Oregon Mist*. He continued to hold a prominent place in political affairs in Oregon for many years as Judge Cleeton.

The second annual teachers' institute in the county was held at Clatskanie the first week in August, 1892, under Superintendent T. J. Cleeton with twenty-five teachers present for most or all of the programs. Tuesday morning was spent in arithmetic, reading and spelling, the afternoon on grammar, history and physiology. The evening had a program of music and Miss Maud Henderson read a paper, "Why I like teaching." This kind of program filled the days, with various hortatory lectures and addresses before the teachers were sent out, inspired and instructed, to fill the schools of the county with eager pupils. Richard H. Bailey of Carico and his son Lester both attended this institute. The institute became an annual feature.

Superintendent J. G. Watts in 1895 listed the various subjects taught in each of the schools in the county: reading, spelling, penmanship, arithmetic, geography, grammar, language, history, physiology. Some of the schools gave instruction in drawing, music, bookkeeping, letter writing, government, morals.

The movement of teachers from school to school indicates the uncertain and tenuous nature of the position. Such an idea as tenure was unheard of and teachers were hired for a term, be it short or long.

Miss Katie A. McGuire finished the summer term at Houlton in September, 1891; moved to the Briggs school for the winter term; and began the spring term at St. Helens on April 11.

Katie McGuire had twenty-eight pupils enrolled at the Briggs school with an average attendance of twenty-three. Some lucky students who were neither absent nor tardy had their names printed in the paper: Charley Gray; Stella Brown; Dannie Brown; Perley Brown (two Brown families were living in the district. Perley's father was Frank Brown, who came from Maine that year. The other Brown father was, probably, Frank's brother.); Sidney and Oliver Smith, children of Amos Alonzo "Lon" Smith, newly come to the Peris area on Smith Creek; Harry, Charley and Pearl Sherman, of the Sherman family from Aroostook county, cousins of the Corliss family; Clarence Beauchamp, son of a minister circuit rider; George Emerson; Ed Stanwood; George Barger. Miss McGuire reported that Mr. Bonney and B. I. Plummer were visitors to her school.

Ernest S. Faxon taught the first of his many terms in the various schools of the area beginning in September, 1893, at the Briggs school. Faxon graduated from Drain Normal School, taking his diploma in June, 1895. In October, 1895, the young Iris Tarbell, writing to her Aunt Anna in Maine, said, "Mr. Faxon who taught three terms here awhile ago is to teach again. He has been in Southern Oregon the past year attending normal school. He is going to have a bookkeeping class and I am going to study . . . . I am anxious to begin."

Young Faxon was son of the Columbia City minister who preached in Yankton frequently. He took an active part in Yankton community affairs, debating in the Literary society, serving as officer in the grange, speaking to the Farmers' Alliance. He married Mrs. Lizzie Sherman on February 11, 1897, with the Rev. C. N. Plowman officiating. Lizzie Faxon served Yankton both as school clerk and postmistress while her husband taught in Yankton, Bachelor Flat and other schools. He was again the "capable and popular teacher" of the Yankton school in 1903 and 1904. Lizzie Sherman Faxon died and he married Julia VanDolah, daughter of a Yankton family, September 1, 1909, the Rev. Gordon C. Barger officiating.

In April, 1911, Julia Faxon gave birth to a nine pound girl. She died of peritonitis a few days later, age 22, and is buried in the Yankton cemetery. That summer Ernest Faxon moved into Houlton to be both principal and superintendent of the Houlton school. A reporter wrote, "He will be a good one. One does not have to be in the Professor's company long to learn that he is a livewire and a born leader." Within the year Faxon resigned because of ill health and moved to California. He was well liked in south Columbia county.

The spring term of 1895 was taught commendably by Miss Marie Watts of the well-known pioneer family of Scappoose. The close of the term at the end of July featured a basket picnic for pupils and parents in the grove, with a program of recitations. Performances were given by, among others, Harold Brown, Ray Tarbell, Charley Brown, Guy Tarbell and Mrs. Cora Barger. Cora Tarbell Barger was an example of a married woman (or girl) attending the country school. She was married at age 14 in April to G. W. Barger, with the written approval of her father, Lawrence Tarbell. Her son was born in October of that year.

Also on the school program that July day was Alta Oliver, the only girl among a family of nine brothers, children of Rose and Samuel Oliver. The Olivers had left Kansas in 1888 and had been in Cowlitz county, Washington, near Woodland. Rose Oliver bought 39 acres on Milton creek near the schoolhouse in 1891 for $800 from Charles Muckle.

Various school districts had problems of finance or personnel, problems sometimes dividing the residents into sharply antagonistic camps. Such a personality clash occurred in Rainier where, when a school director was elected another promptly resigned, asserting that he could not and would not work with that man. Quarrels over whether a teacher should or should not be returned for another term erupted with more or less animosity in some districts. Woe to the director who put a relative to teach in the district.

The county had school funds which were distributed to districts on the basis of school age population. Such funds were usually turned over to school clerks twice a year from the office of the county school superintendent. As supplemental support to the schools a district could levy a property tax. Such school taxes in the 1890s ranged around five mills on assessed property valuation for the entire county average, but districts varied widely on their amount.

John Wilwerding attended a school meeting in the Carico district in March, 1893, proposing a ten mill school tax for the district. Richard H. Bailey was the highly respected teacher, teaching eleven pupils. Mr. Wilwerding's motion was voted down five to two. Someone else proposed a five mill tax, which was approved five to two. The St. Helens district school ran into financial problems and closed in February, 1894, for lack of funds. The district vote was eleven to eight against any tax. The schoolhouse was empty until the second week in September when R. S. Hatton was employed as teacher and school was opened on short notice to the community. Attendance was small for the opening. On Tuesday, March 12, 1895, Mr. Hatton finished his contract term in the school, having had 49 pupils, twenty boys and twenty-nine girls. The clerk reported $28.08 on hand in the treasury. Probably the county funds came through, for Mrs. Bell Gaddis began a three months term on April 2. Mrs. Gaddis returned to teach the St. Helens school in the fall term, beginning in October. In the spring she moved to the Reuben district school.

The fact that M. C. Case had finished his third successive term as teacher in the Houlton school was news. Even more outstanding was his seventeen year record of averaging ten months of teaching each year — a remarkable achievement covering 1879 to 1896.

C. E. Lake was the subject of a considerable community protest in 1909 in the Yankton district. The *Oregon Mist* headed a paragraph: ''Want their teacher — notwithstanding the fact that Mr. C. E. Lake, primary teacher of the

Yankton school fell down on theory and practice in the teachers' examination, he has given excellent satisfaction to the patrons and pupils and they have petitioned the school superintendent to permit him to complete his term. Mr. S. Saulser circulated a petition this week and secured nearly 200 signers endorsing Mr. Lake highly.'' Mr. Lake did finish his term and another year also.

The Yankton people planned a celebration for the Fourth of July, 1902, raising a flag on a new flagpole on the school grounds. The contribution list was:

Guy Tarbell	$1.00
Frank Brown	.50
Lawrence Tarbell	.50
Sardin Saulser	.50
Charles Briggs	.50
Fred Briggs	.50
George Hyde	.50
Ray Tarbell	.50
J. A. Wikstrom	.50
Rudolph Kappler	.50
Eber Brown	.50
Perley Crouse	.50
M. A. Kale	.50
Harry Oliver	.50
(Paid by C. Brown)	
S. S. Way	.25
Mrs. Charlton	.25
L. Plowman	.25
Cornelius Moyer	.25
Louis F. Barger	.25
J. N. Brinn	.25
Perley Brown	.50

At least seven of these contributors had been students in the school.

One set of school statistics reveals the strength of the Milton creek watershed in population, the number of legal school voters. Yankton had 40 legal school voters in 1903, 52 in 1904, 51 in 1905, 45 in 1906, 38 in 1907, 55 in 1908, and 54 in 1909. Peris, #43, had 9 legal school voters in 1902, 6 in 1903, 6 in 1904, 6 in 1905, 5 in 1906, 4 in 1907, 4 in 1908, 7 in 1909.

Valley district #41 had 12 voters in 1903, 12 in 1904, 6 in 1905, 8 in 1906, 5 in 1908; then the school was abandoned. The Trenholm school filled in the area.

Carico district #34 fluctuated from 15 to 30 in school census, from 19 to 4 in school enrollment, and from 19 to 12 legal school voters. School was kept there successively: 7 months, 5, 3½, 4, 7, 7½, 6, 8½, 9 from 1902 through 1910.

The financial problems facing America and the tight money situation in the county reduced teacher salaries during the mid-1890s. The 1896 average salary in the county was $35 a month, down ten dollars since 1892, for the male teachers, while the female teachers averaged $33.01 a month, a drop of $5.49. The average salary for the teaching women dropped again in 1897, to $32.57, while the men's salaries held at $35. Even with the McKinley prosperity giving a boost to the county, teacher salaries remained very low.

The county had 57 district schools in 1901, employed 73 teachers for 1658 pupils. Men's salaries averaged $36.61 a month, women's $33.58. The county had few male teachers.

With the 1900s the salaries particularly for men began a slow improvement: men averaged $41.50, women $33.85. The Warren district paid a man and a woman the same, each fifty dollars a month. Rainier, Neer City, and district 28 each paid women forty dollars a month. Seven districts paid them less than thirty, with three districts paying $25. Fifteen districts paid $30. The eleven male teachers in the county that year varied from $31.50 to $50, with three receiving the fifty.

The July, 1907, report was that the six male teachers in the county averaged $65 while the 95 women teachers averaged $45. School teachers were reported to be scarce. "Half the schools in the Nehalem valley are without teachers."

The 1910 figures show a modest increase, men averaging $71, women $58. Three districts — Clatskanie, Scappoose, Rainier — paid men teachers a hundred dollars a month. St.

Helens paid $80, Warren $75, Houlton $70. Fifteen men taught school in the county that year, one in Shiloh Basin for $56.25 a month. Women ranged from a low of $40 to a high of $70. Ten of the women teachers received $60 or more.

A longer school year was in use by 1910, sixteen of the districts reporting nine months of school. Only three admitted to less than six months of school. The county had a school age population between four and twenty years of 3202 persons, 2159 of them registered in school. Rainier had 292 pupils. Clatskanie 275, Scappoose 173, St. Helens 157, Quincy 110, Warren 104, Houlton 101. Thirty of the districts had fewer than 25 pupils registered, with eight districts having fewer than ten pupils.

In September 1911 four high schools in the county had a total enrollment of less than a hundred pupils. Rainier had 35, Clatskanie 32, St. Helens 17, thirteen of them first year students, and Scappoose had thirteen high school students.

VI: MILTON CREEK FACES UP TO HARD TIMES

*Alterations of Times and Customs branch them into so
many parts that there's no arguing from what has been
to what may be now.*

Don Quixote

The early years of the 1890s were economically troubled
and difficult times for Americans. The spirit of hope and
expectation which had pervaded the entire country for most
of a century had received reverses during the 1870s and
1880s; but during the early 1890s panic and fear were
widespread following bank failures, shortage of money,
closing factories, falling prices for farm produce, violent
strikes and civil disorder. Distrust of power and privilege
were rising and more farmers were following the advice to
quit growing corn and raise hell. Grain was being burned
because it had no market value. Barter was replacing
money, because money was unavailable. "Spuds and
shingles are legal tender" in Apiary, wrote the
correspondent for the *Oregon Mist*. The national industrial
and monetary system was faltering as it almost ceased to
function.

The picture of the American farmer or worker "quietly
but surely threading his way from poverty and toil to certain
competence if not wealth," as Horace Greeley had phrased
it, was fading from the American scene. *The Autobiography
of William Allen White* gives his personal observations on
the rise of the Farmers' Alliance in the Kansas farm country
as a protest movement, even while "the bankers, the
lawyers, the good deacons of the churches who passed the

hat, and the Past Grands or the Noble Knights in the lodges" still laughed at what these prideful ones considered the dregs and the rabble rousers. White wrote of how these shabbily dressed older men of the Farmers' Alliance who were struggling against difficult times goaded him into writing his fiery editorial, "What's the Matter with Kansas?" which became a showpiece and rallying cry for the hopeful believers in the American future. White ridiculed the protesters and called for the solid virtues on which the republic was grounded. He saw a Kansas where people were "fleeing from it by the score every day, capital going out of the state by the hundreds of dollars; and every industry but farming paralyzed, and that crippled . . ." because laboring men could not buy the produce. He answered his question by implication: What is needed is less protest and more work. What's the matter with Kansas? "Kansas is all right. There is absolutely nothing wrong with Kansas. 'Every prospect pleases and only man is vile.'"

White undoubtedly never heard of the Milton creek valley and it is probable that very few settlers of this western timbered country read or even heard of White's catchy editorial, but the principles on which White was resting his view of man's plight were known and appreciated in Columbia county. During this period of national concern over the economy and the structure of society the Milton creek settlers worked on, doing the best they could, making do with what they had; if they were protesting, not protesting over much. They were building a community in the West despite obstacles and hardship. The spirit of hope and expectation continued to prevail. The potato crop might come short of expectation or potatoes might be dirt cheap, but a Deer Island writer to the *Oregon Mist* expressed the prevailing feeling of the county.

"Hard times are rough on the common laborer, who must buy all the necessities of his existence, but the economical farmer who keeps out of debt is safe and hard times to him are like 'water on a duck's back,' and especially in a year like the past one, when crops are so abundant."

The Milton creek area with its logging operations and its few sawmills and shingle mills had various laborers coming and going as the operations closed down or opened, but most of the people in the valley were attached to land and worked out when work was available as an added activity. No resident of the valley had job security, an annual income, or sufficient means to live without additional labor.

Timber was the source of income in this country. The Northern Pacific railroad and the creeks flowing into the river were outlets for the logs and wood products. The harvesting of this resource of trees proceeded at an uneven pace. The owners of the timber and the logging operators and mill owners were hostage to the weather and the roads, the availability of orders, boxcars, and river shipping, and the fluctuations of the market. No mill or logging operation worked steadily. Neither did any close down for long.

In this valley and in this decade no absentee owner financed timber operations. Every mill owner and logging operator worked with his men in a small crew. Howard's mill and the Muckle Brothers logging operation probably each employed eight or ten men when in operation. Other projects were smaller in scope. Cordwood cutting was one of the principal labor-using activities. The railroad used wood for its locomotives. The steamboats burned wood. Both railroad cars and boats hauled cordwood to Portland where, in October, 1891, it sold readily for two dollars a cord. Sometimes Milton creek ran full with cordwood. Cordwood was hauled from Bunker Hill and piled beside the railroad track or on a wharf for shipment. Oregon used 482,254 cords of fuel wood in 1880, and the yearly consumption increased over the next two decades. Columbia county produced a large share of that cordwood.

In April, 1898, the Oregon Wood Company sold 500 cords of wood from their St. Helens wharf to steamboats, getting from $1.50 to $2 a cord for it delivered to the wharf. The cutters were receiving from eighty to ninety cents a cord, but were asking for $1.15.

In June, 1892, Herb Howard was reported to be shipping two carloads of lumber a day from Houlton. This was journalistic exaggeration, or a short term estimate. At the same time the Emerson and Bailey shingle mill was shipping a like amount of shingles. Howard's mill was, however, soon closed down for a time, as the reporter for September 9 wrote, "H. O. Howard has started up his mill again and is evidently intending to make a long run." Alonzo A. Smith's logging operation at Peris, after being closed a year, was beginning operation again, while the camp of Stanwood and Holstein was being shut down. The Emerson Brothers shingle mill ran a week at the end of July. Lumber was offered at four dollars a thousand, off a dollar or more.

The panic of 1893 shook the country. The editor of the *Oregon Mist*, May 12, expressed the uneasiness of the times. "Indications point to a light season with the logging camps so far as the prospect for making sales of logs is concerned. It is expected, however, that some lumber will be manufactured but it is not thought the cut will more than supply the local demand . . . . It is hoped that some unforeseen influence will soon make its appearance and revive the lumber market, as this enterprise is necessary to the prosperity of business on the lower Columbia."

Horace Greeley traveled over Kansas in 1859 and wrote, "It takes three log cabins to make a city in Kansas." In the inner Columbia county of 1890 the cabins were more likely to be of split cedar than of logs, but it didn't take many settlers to get a name, a post office, and a school. Carico opened a post office on December 3, 1889, with Lydia Pinckney, wife of the storekeeper Nelson Pinckney, as postmistress.

Christopher Sauervein's first newsworthy achievement was falling into the thirty-six-foot well he was digging, getting more wet than seriously injured. He opened a country store and opened the Peris post office in his store, serving as postmaster for a year before he resigned that appointment and closed his store. Solomon Rock was carrying the mail three times a week over the road where the mud was boottop deep. Sauervein, unable to find work near home, worked in Portland, coming home for visits in October 1893 and February, March and June, 1894.

The little settlements between Pittsburg and the Briggs school developed in the late 1880s-'90s with a surprising endurance of a few hardy settlers. Enough details have survived the years to indicate how the various families faced the undeveloped land and the economically troubled times.

Richard Bailey, a farmer, logger, school teacher, weathered the 1890s by doing some farming on his acres and taking orders for nursery stock for a Portland nursery. He taught his local school when it was first opened, taught a five month term at the Briggs school, logged with Alonzo Smith, and taught the Vernonia school. Mrs. Bailey and Mrs. Pope went hop-picking in August, 1895. Bailey was road supervisor for the Houlton district in 1898 and 1899. In April, 1900, he and J. N. "Nick" Brinn opened a store in Houlton.

Leslie Bailey married Winnie Emerson, age sixteen, on August 14, 1888. In 1892 he and his brother-in-law Fred Emerson started a shingle mill at Peris. Soon Bailey was running the little mill alone; but it did not last long. He went hop-picking in 1894 and then worked for his one-time brother-in-law Herb Howard in Howard's sawmill. Mrs. Bailey cooked for the Howard boarding house. The eight-year-old son of the Baileys, Willie, while playing in the mill, had his clothing catch on the machinery and was badly mangled in a quick death in August, 1896. A lubricating glass exploded near Bailey's eye in Howard's mill in February, 1897. His eye was removed in a Portland hospital. He later became a bartender.

Cornelius C. Moyer was working on the Columbia river for the Bridal Veil Lumber Company when he came home for a birthday party in September, 1891. Moyer farmed, worked out, tended road, built his house, taught school, and sent his two children, Willie and Kissie, to Willamette University in Salem. He was one of the dependable and admired residents of the valley.

Solomon Rock, a bachelor, homesteaded in the Carico valley in 1879. He donated an acre of land for the Peris school district, #43, and served as clerk of the district. He worked at logging and farming, logging for J. N. Brinn at various times. He carried the Peris mail. He drove ox team for Herb Howard. He was notable for his devoted work on the public road. He lived to be 82 years old, dying at Columbia City in June, 1929.

The Seth Pope family were early settlers in the county. Seth was the county judge for a time during the 1850s, and he was active in St. Helens and county affairs. His son, B. F. Pope, settled on a farm at Peris which he improved and developed while he was working as a logger or in Howard's sawmill. The Pope farm was said to have the finest view in the district, a view over the Cascade mountain peaks of St. Helens, Adams and Hood, and the Washington lower hills. He could see the steamboats on the Columbia river from his farm.

Deeper into the interior county was another settlement which took the post office name Valley. Joseph Dupont settled on his homestead about 1890, a year or so before John Wilwerding filed for his claim. Wilwerding's three brothers-in-law, the Karths — John, William and Rudolph — were planting crops before 1892. Farther into the interior at Apiary the few settlers clammored for a sawmill, and one was started in 1891. It had been cutting lumber only a few weeks before it had labor problems. The men working protested that twenty dollars a month was not enough pay, so most of them quit.

Farmers, however, needed some cash and would work. Laura Briggs rode horseback the twenty or more miles to the settlements on the river to carry in family provisions on a pack horse. The Millers, William and Wilfred, grew tobacco on their farm. Many settlers were doing building on their farms, sometimes with hand split cedar lumber; slashing, burning and clearing land was general.

B. F. Pope built a two-story barn with a steep enough roof to hold up under the weight of snow or slide it off. It snowed five feet deep in the winter of 1892-93, and repeated it the next winter. The Brinns built a new home. Rudolph Kappler built a fine new home. J. R. Sherman built a new barn. Alonzo A. "Lon" Smith built the largest barn in the area around Smith creek.

Catherine (Mrs. Joseph) Dupont

The Valley district was getting new settlers with names and backgrounds different from the Maine and Michigan settlers further down Milton creek. Valentine Gliniecki sponsored the building of the St. Joseph Polish Catholic church. People with names like Febuski, Dalatski, Sintak, Lintek, Kineski, Wisnoski, Coboski, Ramblaski, Sobieski, Walezek, claimed their farms and dug into the land. James Gaitena had a daughter, two or three years old, catch her clothing on fire and die from the burns. John Wilwerding was said to own the finest horse in the county and William Karth sported a fine horse and buggy which he bought from I. G. Wikstrom. Ole Erickson contributed the acre of ground for the Valley school. J. Sintak built a fine residence. Joseph Deleski went to Scappoose to work on West's dairy farm. His father T. Deleski built a large barn. Andrew Wisnoski moved from Rainier to his ranch in Valley. He and Joseph Deleski took a contract to clear land for Thomas Holstein. Anton Kerowski settled on his homestead in section 26 by 1895. He proved up on the land in April, 1901, his witnesses being Steve Lampa and William Karth.

The Frank Sobieski family settled on land high on Bunker Hill, farming, and with Frank working some in logging. In 1895 he was well enough known as a responsible resident to be appointed road supervisor for his district by the county commissioners. His children went to the Valley school. A Catholic family, they were part of the St. Joseph Polish Catholic church parish, the church which Valentine Gliniecki had promoted.

The August 10, 1894, *Oregon Mist* carried a news item: "Criminal assault — Last Friday one Sibiski living out in the Poland settlement came into town and stated that one Glineski had found Mrs. Sibiski in a berry patch and struck her several blows with a club, finally knocking her down, after which he began choking her until two other women near by interfered. Sibiski went to Reuben and swore out a warrant for Glineski's arrest, which was served Saturday. He was taken before Justice Brown, and placed under bond to appear tomorrow for trial. There seems to have been an old grievance about land which prompted the assault."

The August 17 follow-up item read: "After many witnesses had been examined sustaining a great deal of expense, the court imposed a fine of $5 and costs upon the defendant." Another news item in the same paper was that Mrs. Sibiski was again able to attend to household duties.

This is not the last appearance in the news of Columbia county of these two families. Valentine Gliniecki was seeking support from his neighbors for the position of road supervisor in 1897, but he did not get the appointment. His son Frank Gliniecki, who bought part of his father's farm and built his own home, shot a three hundred pound bear in August, 1900. The next month events piled up on Valentine

Gliniecki. His house on Bunker Hill burned to the ground and he was taken to a hospital in Portland with a badly infected left foot. The doctors amputated his leg at the knee. Frank Gliniecki soon moved to St. Helens to work.

Frank Sobieski was severely injured at work by a large log rolling on him in February, 1897. He was taken in a sleigh to his home and a doctor was sent for. Two weeks later he was reported to be at least partially paralyzed from the accident. His son Joe continued the work on the farm, doing spring plowing. The same issue of the *Oregon Mist* which reported the amputation of Gliniecki's leg reported that Frank Sobieski was able to hobble around on crutches. In November, 1899, the daughter Nettie had to give up her work in Portland and come home to care for her ill parents. Joe Sobieski continued to farm in Valley for a few years, but by the spring of 1904 the Sobieski family were on a farm on Tedford creek above the Yankton school, near the dam which Muckle had mentioned in deeding land to J. N. Brinn.

Disaster happened fast for the Sobieski family. Frank Sobieski, overcome with despair from constant pain and helplessness, slashed his throat in an unsuccessful attempt to end his life. The Sobieski daughter Jessie came home from Portland where she was working to be with the family during its anquish. Friends gathered around the Sobieski home on the Fourth of July. Eva Sobieski, fifteen years old, was wading in the Tedford creek dam when in the soft mud she got in over her head. John, age 13, and Augusta Jessie, age 24, went to her rescue but in the treacherous mud bottom of the creek all three lost their lives. Cassilda Wilwerding was at the Sobieski home when that tragic event happened and many years later impressed the magnitude of the disaster upon her daughter. The three children were buried in the Yankton cemetery which a Catholic priest from Portland consecrated for them.

The Karth brothers sent a letter from the Yukon to the *Oregon Mist*, which had started a fund to help care for the extra Sobieski expenses: "We all feel sorry for the Sobieski family, we have known them for fourteen years. They have been the very best friends to us and we know their faithfulness." The two Karth men sent $30, their sister Rosie $25, Ole Kuinie $5, Mrs. Brandmeyer $5. In all, sixty-five dollars came from the Yukon to help the stricken family on Tedford creek.

Nettie Sobieski worked in Portland for a time and then returned to Yankton to marry Steve Lampa in October, 1906. Lampa built a house on land on the Pittsburg road half a mile above the Yankton school. It is the Lampa place to this day. In 1907 the Sobieski parents went to live in the Lampa home. Another Sobieski daughter married John Walczak of Valley. Joe Sobieski married Mary Jane Boylen, who bore him four daughters: Harriet, Agnes, Grace, Patricia.

Joe Sobieski continued to farm above Yankton. In May, 1911, an unfortunate incident involved him in the news. He was giving a ride in his wagon to Charles Bumgartner, an epileptic alcoholic. Charles was said to have been drunk for a week. He fell from Sobieski's wagon near the Sobieski farm and though the Sobieskis gave him what assistance they could, he died within a few hours. The coroner's verdict said that death was due to prolonged alcoholism.

The Karths, from Germany, settled in Minnesota and then came to Oregon in the late 1880s. Caroline Karth, the mother of seven children, was born in 1829 and died at Bunker Hill west of Trenholm July 22, 1895. She was buried in the St. Joseph cemetery. Caroline's sons William and Rudolph, twins born November 10, 1863, and John, a little older, came to settle on homesteads about 1890. Her daughter Matilda married John Baptiste Wilwerding, a native of Luxembourg, in Minnesota, where their eldest daughter Ida was born at Wionoa in 1886. The Wilwerdings came first to Portland and then settled on the homestead at the top of the hill west of Trenholm, where Wilwerding lived the rest of his life. This Wilwerding hill entered frequently into the discussion of the St. Helens-Pittsburg road.

The Karth and Wilwerding families were frequently mentioned in the local news of the county, for civic activities, for fine oats or potatoes on their farms, for fine horses to drive and for their working in different places logging or carpentering in between farm seasons. When the Yukon

John Wilwerding on his homestead.

gold fever struck, John and Rudolph Karth headed for gold country, spending eight years up north, with several extended visits home. The Karth men could show gold nuggets to their neighbors as evidence of their success. William visited his brothers up north in 1905, possibly thinking of settling there; however he returned, bought a farm at Yankton, built a house and barn and soon married. Rudolph also returned to Yankton, bought a farm, married and remained in Yankton until his death in 1947. Neither of the Karth twins had children. Their brother John visited in Minnesota, worked around Columbia county, and went to Saskatchawan to homestead in August, 1914. Matilda and John Wilwerding had three daughters: Ida, who died of pneumonia in 1920 at age 33; Cassilda "Cassie," born October 29, 1888; and Mary, born 1893 and died December 1, 1919. Cassie lived until 1975.

Wilwerding's homestead paper signed with Grover Cleveland's name is dated November 6, 1896, just as McKinley was elected the next president. Wilwerding took up his homestead in 1891, moved his family to the ranch in March, 1892. The family returned to Portland in May, and then back to the farm in November. Matilda died giving birth to a child in 1896. She as a Lutheran was denied the right to be buried in the St. Joseph cemetery and her grave was prepared outside, but within a few feet of her mother Caroline's. Wilwerding, a skilled craftsman and carpenter, erected an impressive headpiece of cedar for his wife's grave.

John Wilwerding

Wilwerding left his mark upon the Oregon landscape, for it was he who sent to Scotland for Scotchbroom seed. He kept bees and he thought the Scotchbroom would further his bee culture. He made his hives of hand split cedar. Wilwerding lost two houses by fire and built his own cabin, making his furniture. His granddaughter Cassilda in Beaverton still has in use some of that furniture. The Wilwerding daughters went to the Peris school where Wilwerding served as a director. Cassie kept a fragmentary diary at times, writing, "Daddy married to Mrs. Eder at St. Marys church half past eight. Mass." That was December 31, 1908. Stephanie Eder Wilwerding urged her husband repeatedly to move to Portland, but he stuck to his cabin at the top of Wilwerding hill west of Trenholm. The Karths moved to Yankton. The Duponts moved away. The community around the Catholic church all left. But John Wilwerding remained on his hilltop farm.

William and Wilford Miller sold their Valley farm at the end of the decade and moved to a farm near St. Helens. Joseph Dupont, in addition to farming, opened a shingle mill with the new century. He ran an active mill, cutting fifteen to twenty thousand shingles a day for several years; but he was a long way from market. Mrs. Dupont was the postmistress at Valley.

In June, 1896, the Valley school had nine boys and ten girls enrolled. Those with perfect attendance for the month were Rose and Leontine Dupont, Martha and John Sintek, Katie and Mattie Dalatski, and Sofa and Conrad Ramblaski. Leontine Dupont became ill with malignant diptheria at the end of March, 1901. After a week the doctor was brought out to see her, but she died on Tuesday, April 2, and was buried in the St. Joseph cemetery.

On August 16, 1981, Frank Reed of Vernonia took the author to the site of the St. Joseph Polish Catholic church and cemetery. One of the persons buried there was Helen Osmialowski, the sister of Robert Rydzewski, Frank Reed's father. Helen died a few days after the birth of her daughter Stella in 1905. The attractive small building used for a school, a Sunday school and a church, burned from a slashing fire out of control on August 4, 1899, and was never rebuilt. The cemetery was used for burial for a few people after the church was gone, but it, too, was abandoned. Today the entire area for miles around is given over to timber, the young firs of twenty to forty years covering the hills and valleys as far as one can see. All attempts at farming the area have long been abandoned.

The land which was once the St. Joseph church site was sold to Robert Reed (he had changed his name from the Polish Rydzewski) in 1924 by the Portland archdiocese. Frank Reed as a boy lived there and became familiar with the people and past of the area. The cemetery was hidden in the trees and undergrowth, grown high with ferns, briars, salal brush and grass when the author visited there in 1981. Only two grave stones were still in evidence, one marking the grave of Caroline Karth 1829-1896, with Henry Grinka 1881-1897, her grandson, also on the same stone. The other, some twenty feet away, marked the burial place of the twelve-year-old Leontine Dupont, daughter of Joseph and Catharine Dupont. Four or five feet from the Karth headstone were the remnants of the cedar marker lovingly crafted by John Wilwerding to mark the grave of his wife Matilda.

Frank Reed also took the author a mile or two away to the grave of August Schieve, the only man ever hanged by law in Columbia county. Schieve was publicly hanged in the courthouse yard in St. Helens on July 2, 1902. He was buried on the Schieve farm, fifty feet from where the Schieve farm-house stood. Reed remembered seeing a picket fence around the single grave. When he was a boy, a little fir tree grew in the small enclosure. Now the picket fence is gone and the fir tree is four or five feet in diameter and a hundred and fifty feet tall, the biggest, oldest tree in the area, left by loggers to mark the grave of August Schieve, hanged for a murder he may not have committed.

As Frank Reed told the story, August's father, on his deathbed, confessed that he, John Schieve, had murdered Joseph Schulkowski on December 26, 1901. Joseph Schulkowski boarded in the Schieve home, even courted the

John Wilwerding crafted this grave marker for his wife Matilda's grave. She died in 1896, the year he proved up on his homestead. The grave is in the overgrown and neglected St. Joseph Catholic cemetery near Trenholm. Remnants of the cedar marker were still evident in 1982.

Schieve daughter — attention the father had disapproved. Schulkowski was selling his land, had money in a moneybelt and was leaving the area when he was murdered on the Bunker Hill road and his body dumped behind a log. The Schieve horse and Schieve gun were implicated in the murder. The jury considered for fourteen hours before finding August Schieve guilty on circumstantial evidence. August Schieve professed his innocence to the end. Frank Reed said, "The neighbors hanged August Schieve. They did not like him, for various petty reasons. August was playing cards with my father and another man on the day of the murder. They were not called as witnesses. Various neighbors testified that Schieve was the kind of man who might commit murder for money. They just didn't like him." Some forty residents of the area testified at the trial. Reed said that the father let his own son be hanged for the murder he had committed.

The *Oregon Mist* issues for July 4, 1902, and July 11, 1902, have accounts of the hanging and a summary of the events leading up to the hanging. The headline was "Schieve is Dead/Protested That He Was Innocent." The prisoner did not flinch or cower, but walked steadily and firmly up the thirteen steps to the scaffold. The Reverend Lew Davies, Methodist minister for St. Helens and Rainier, was on the scaffold with him, as was Schieve's uncle Carl Schieve from Portland, and two German ministers from Portland. Reverend Davies said a prayer before the sheriff gave the fatal signal. Schieve's father John Schieve was in the enclosure to witness the hanging along with two hundred spectators.

The murder had been committed on December 26, 1901. August Schieve was arraigned and charged on April 12, 1902, after the district attorney had questioned as witnesses Adolph Schieve, John Schieve, August Schieve, Eva Zeller, Julius Floeter, Joseph Sobieski, Dr. Edwin Ross, Dr. H. A. Cliff, Sheriff R.S. Hatton, J.B. Godfrey, W.A. Wood, Joseph Nitch — the latter three the discoverers of the corpse. August Schieve was represented by attorney W. T. Vaughn.

For the trial, which began May 15 and concluded on May 24, the following persons were added to the witness list of the court: E. T. Gore, O. D. Garrison, J. D. McKay, Mrs. Frank Gliniecki, A. King, James Spence, C. H. Briggs, Gus Sanberg, Gus Bus, E. C. Dalton, Frank George, Fred Watkins, A.F. Leonard, August G. Spekarth, W.W. Blakesley, J. H. Wellington, H. P. Ford, J. L. Lambersen.

The nature of the testimony given is not available. This array of witnesses included St. Helens business people, laborers, public officials, as well as some residents of the Valley area.

Schieve was held in jail in Portland "for safety" between his arraignment and the trial. After his sentencing to death by hanging, a petition was prepared by James A. Ray and

Sheriff R. S. Hatton. Forty signatures were on the petition to Governor T.T. Geer, asking him to change the sentence to imprisonment. Governor Geer took no action; he was involved in other problems, having just been defeated in his try for reelection.

Sheriff Hatton had troubled his conscience over his prisoner during the long months since Schieve had first been implicated and detained for questioning. Hatton's early feelings had been that Schieve was innocent of the murder, but by the time of the hanging he felt that Schieve had committed the murder but should not be hanged. Schieve's mother had been since his early boyhood an inmate of the Oregon State Hospital. A reporter for the *Oregon Statesman* wrote, "Sheriff Hatton made a special study of the man and believed that his brain was abnormally developed, that while he was bright in some respects, he was mentally unbalanced in others . . . Sheriff Hatton also believed that Schieve was lacking in the sensations of sorrow, remorse, regard for truth, etc. . . ."

The *Oregonian* on June 30 had a brief report from St. Helens: "Everything is now in readiness [for the hanging] . . . Undertaker George made the coffin that is to hold the remains of the murderer . . . Schieve doggedly contends that he is innocent of the murder . . . Schieve's father has been in town during the past three days, and asserts that his son did not commit the murder."

A further report on the day before the hanging said that Schieve was somewhat nervous, for the first time. "It is expected that the county authorities will take charge of the body after the execution and bury it in the pauper plot in the Germany Hill cemetery; as Schieve's relatives have not expressed any desire to attend to the interment . . . after death shall have taken place."

The *Oregonian*, with a photograph of Schieve, gave an extended report on the hanging, as did the *Oregon Statesman* and the *Oregon Mist*. The three accounts furnish different details and have one significant variation.

A large fenced enclosure surrounded the gallows, an area large enough to hold the 200 persons who had been invited to attend. Two of the accounts say that the father was in the enclosure and witnessed the hanging, but the most detailed account, and probably in this instance the more accurate, that in the *Oregon Statesman*, reports that the father was with his son for a moment to say goodbye and then asked to be let out of the enclosure.

Schieve was given the opportunity to make a statement from the scaffold, and he spoke in a firm voice, protesting his innocence. "He stated that he saw several of the jurymen who convicted him among the crowd, and witnesses who testified against him, but he forgave them all.

"'Gentlemen,' said the prisoner, 'I suppose many people have hard feelings toward me. Some of the people cast the votes. I know they think I am guilty, but I am innocent. I don't wish any of you people hard luck.'"

A slight rain was falling, the scene was dismal to the highest degree. Schieve was a trifle emotional but only for a short time. "He declared his father . . . was the murderer of the ex-soldier . . ."

When he had finished speaking, the guard stood ready beside him. "'So long, Joe,' 'So Long, Leopold.' Such were the cheery salutations in a tremulous voice sung out before 200 spectators by August Schieve as the black cap was adjusted over his head. 'Goodbye, Uncle,' he said." The Rev. Davies said a prayer before the sheriff gave the fateful signal. Twelve minutes after the fall broke Schieve's neck the group of physicians in attendance pronounced August Schieve dead.

The law asked that twelve electors of the county certify that the judgment of the court was fulfilled. The twelve worthy citizens given that disagreeable task were A. B. Dillard, W. A. Miles, George A. Hall, Martin White, J. B. Godfrey, L. W. VanDyke, Washington Muckle, E. Seffert, F. M. Thorp, H. Morgus, John Gilmore, R. H. Mitchell.

The father and the family took the corpse home for burial on the farm.

Frank Reed, eighty years later, said that the neighbors hanged August Schieve. They did not like him for various

August Schieve, hanged for murder in St. Helens in 1902
Oregonian photo, Oregon Historical Society

petty reasons. The belief that the father was the murderer is widespread in Columbia county.

The Schieves were Russian Polanders who had settled on their land near Valley in 1894. They had not been popular in the community. Joseph Schulkowski, the murdered man, was a Prussian, a veteran from the U. S. Army in the Spanish-American war, who had come to the Valley community upon his discharge from the army and had purchased a homestead relinquishment. He had made his home with the Schieve family.

A dozen feet from the Schieve grave still stands a battered and storm-worn old pear tree, one lone remnant of the orchards planted by the thrifty settlers on this remote Bunker Hill outpost of Columbia county settlements. Frank Reed sold his farm land to a timber company. The people

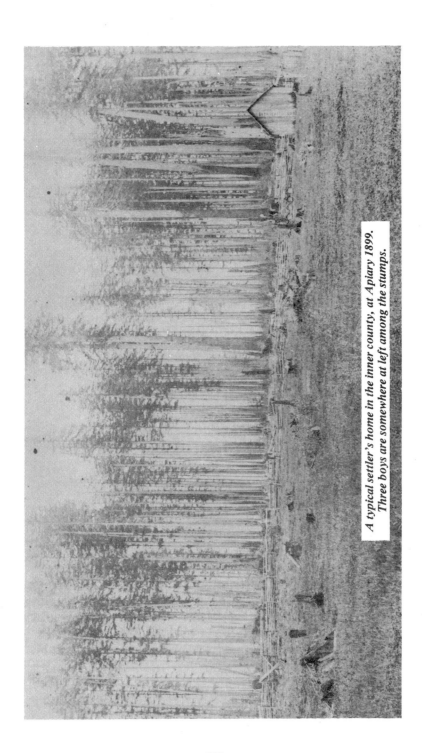

A typical settler's home in the inner county, at Apiary 1899. Three boys are somewhere at left among the stumps.

little by little moved away from this once promising settlement, and gave it back to the trees and shrubs, weeds and grass.

The Peris school held its spring picnic in 1896 in the grove on the R. D. Fowler farm. Twelve students were enrolled in the school, including Cassilda and Ida Wilwerding, William Moyer, William and Alphonse Sauervein, Lester Bailey and Harry Howard, the son of Herb and Molly Howard, reared in the home of Molly and Thomas Holstein.

Slashing was a general activity up and down the valley. One observer estimated that a hundred acres in the Peris area alone was slashed out in the one summer of 1892 and burned over in the fall. The burning of five or ten acres of dried slashing offered a challenge and the possibility of excitement. Usually several men cooperated. The fires were started in several places. Men had shovels, axes, pails of water and wet sacks for use in controlling the fire. The object, of course, was to get as clean a burn as possible. No one knows how many acres of good timber were burned by slashing fires out of control.

Forest fires, however started, were a danger to the farms. In 1895 the William Dearing farm was burned out — home, barn, buildings, fences, crops. Rudolph Karth's barn and hay were burned by a forest fire in July, 1896, which also burned fences and timber on R. McGrew's farm.

Even with the panic of 1893 paralyzing much of the commercial activity of the county, life in this quiet valley went on much as usual. Little indication appeared in the Milton creek valley to indicate that the worst economic crisis to hit the United States of America was passing over the land. The five feet of snow in the upper valley over the winter was causing more talk than the tightness in the sale of logs. The principal indicator of local concern over the economy of the country was the appearance of the Farmers' Alliance.

In August, 1891, the Farmers' Alliance began making its presence known in Columbia county. Professor Rork, state lecturer for the alliance, on a speaking tour of the county spoke in Scappoose, Vernonia, Wilson and Warren, giving the kind of rabble-rousing speech which offended the rational nature of William Allen White of Kansas. Rork's approach went like this: When farmers and laborers organize, a shout of protest goes up that the country is being ruined. People who sound like that are ignorant fools and knaves. The depressed farmer and laborer can get no relief from either of the old political parties. What is demanded is a new approach. Rork from that kind of opening went into an hour and a half analysis of the economic situation of the nation to prove by statistics and logic that the free coinage of silver was necessary under a new government.

The organized chapters of the Farmers' Alliance met for a county-wide meeting in July, 1892. E. D. Darling, the county organizer, was in Yankeetown in May, 1893, to organize the local lodge and supervise the election of lodge officers. Fred Emerson is the only officer mentioned in the report. The chapter was organized with seventeen people present, beginning a period of active growth. The successive reports from the local correspondents at Maineville and Peris indicate the spreading interest in the movement. July 21: "Ten of our citizens joined the Farmers' Alliance here last Saturday night and five others intend joining next Saturday night." August 25: "The Farmers' Alliance at this place initiated six candidates Saturday night."

The Alliance put on a program at the Yankton schoolhouse on Saturday, September 10, an open meeting with a discussion of the question "What is the most profitable crop for the farmers of this vicinity to raise?" The popular teacher Ernest S. Faxon spoke upon the beauties and advantages of rural life and the program also included readings, recitations and music. The next week the school teacher from Pittsburg, William Powell, spoke to the Alliance. Darling of Pittsburg spoke to the Alliance at Yankton on October 15. But interest soon dwindled.

The populist party had elected George Massie sheriff of Columbia county in 1892. This victory at the polls was not an auspicious event for the populist movement, for Massie was an unpopular public official. In a few months he managed to have the tax records in confusion, if not chaos, and he vanished from the county, going first to Canada and then South Africa, with some three thousand or more dollars of county tax funds unaccounted for. The candidates for office on the regular party tickets could point a finger at the fringe parties.

Yet the populist county convention in April, 1896, had Abraham Crouse, the Yankton logger, as a delegate. The Democratic county convention drew an impressive list of delegates from the St. Helens-Milton creek area: Charles E. Emerson; E. A. and C. W. Emerson, sons of Charles; William H. Dolman, the successful businessman and farmer; N. A. Perry, the Houlton postmaster; and Joe Dupont, a farmer from Valley. W. B. Dillard, well-known attorney, and Charles E. Emerson were on the county Democratic steering committee.

The 1894 June election for county officials showed a mixed result, with all three parties placing candidates in office. The People's Party elected a county commissioner and congressman. Fifteen hundred and twelve people cast ballots. The editor of the *Oregon Mist* drew one conclusion from the mixed results of the election: the people of Oregon opposed the gold standard in 1894. Robert G. Smith of Grants Pass, in the spring of 1896, spoke to an overflow crowd at the Yankton school discussing the financial question in detail. He was speaking against the free silver program of Bryan and in favor of the McKinley candidacy.

The fall presidential election gave the state and Columbia county to McKinley, the Republican candidate carrying the county by 193 votes. The St. Helens-Yankton precinct had the largest vote it had ever recorded, 414, with McKinley receiving a 26 vote majority. The more dominantly foreign sections of the county gave Bryan a lead in the precincts of Apiary, Auburn, Beaver Falls and Oak Point. Rainier was a stand-off.

No one denied that times were difficult, money scarce, employment difficult to find, and commerce sluggish during those early years of the 1890s in Columbia county, but no one pushed the panic button. Life went on as smoothly as it could over the muddy ungraded roads which the settlers had to use.

The county in 1894 had 5,890 people, 1,759 of them legal voters. That year the farmers of the county had 12,372 acres of land under cultivation, certainly not all of it cleared of stumps. The potato harvest was 63,284 bushels, and orchards produced 8,235 bushels of apples and pears. The salmon catch in the county was 6,193 barrels. In addition to the logs rafted up the Willamette slough to Multnomah county mills, Columbia county cut 18,176,000 board feet of lumber and 20,000,000 shingles. In lumber cut in the state, Columbia county was second only to Multnomah, but in log production it probably was the leading county.

The presidential campaign in the late summer and early fall of 1896 was one to arouse emotional fervor over the money question and the economic structure of the nation. Vachel Lindsay, a boy in Springfield, Illinois, wrote of his feeling of elation and hopeful excitement as Bryan came to speak in that city. The entire countryside poured into the city to see, to hear, and to chant "Bryan, Bryan, Bryan, Bryan" — as Lindsay named his poem.

Lindsay in that poem captured the feeling that McKinley represented dollar signs, watch chains across overstuffed vests, spats — and old Pierpont Morgan. This was one view of the issues in the election. But it was not the view dominant on Milton creek. In that valley of tall timber the election of McKinley meant that the creek would flow with logs again.

VII: MCKINLEY PROSPERITY COMES TO COLUMBIA COUNTY

To an imagination of any scope the most far-reaching scope of power is not money, it is the command of ideas.

January 8, 1897
Justice Oliver Wendell Holmes

The Yankton notes in the *Oregon Mist* for November 27, 1896, represent the tone of the remaining years of the decade. The writer expresses a deep conviction which permeated this new settlement. Not only is the literary society prospering: the timber industry also is beginning a new and brisk movement. "We can hear again the whistle of Muckle Brothers' logging donkey, which was silent a long time before the election, and which goes to prove that logging is again starting up on this creek." Moreover: "Since the election of McKinley, Mr. H.O. Howard anticipates running his mill all winter, with an increased force of men." By December 10 Howard had four teams hauling lumber, ties and logs for his busy operation. Henry Burnett drove a team of horses, Solomon Rock an ox team. Alfred Harrison, James Cox and George Brous were employed, Brous as head sawyer.

The forecasts of rising prosperity made a few days after the defeat of Bryan and free silver, and with the promise of McKinley stability, were fulfilled over the coming years. Forests were more rapidly being floated down the creek. Donkey engines gradually replaced teams of oxen; the prices paid for logs and lumber rose perceptibly; the roads little by little become more useable; the population increased with new settlers. Farms were cleared, orchards planted, cattle herds improved, houses and barns built and improved. And Yankton was at last blessed with a general country store.

"The buzz of the shingle mill is again heard in our town," wrote a correspondent from Clatskanie. The shingle mills were mostly busy in the new era of prosperity. Nehalem sawmills were running. W. K. Tichenor and three or four other teamsters were hauling lumber to the river, making a procession almost every day through Clatskanie. River traffic was on the increase.

The New York *Tribune* on March 5, 1897, expressed the hopeful note for much of the nation: "Republicans take the helm. Under bright skies and with fair winds, the ship of state sails for the haven of prosperity." Columbia county was but joining in the general feeling of exultation.

After McKinley was well established in office and the country was on an even keel under his leadership, the feeling of "McKinley Prosperity" was still finding expression: "James Spence is kept busy all the time shoeing horses, repairing wagons, etc. Even the 'village blacksmith' feels the quickened pulse of business conditions, attributable to the fact that a good McKinley guides the destinies of states."

The editor of the *Oregon Mist* was still bullish on Columbia county as the decade moved toward its close: "That Columbia county has a bright future in store is a statement that needs no assurance. The magnificence of her agricultural resources, with the wealth of the many thousands of acres of splendid timber . . . means that an era of prosperity is setting in . . . The wealth is about us and needs but to be developed."

Everyone knew that the land needed a lot of developing to realize its potential. The editor recognized that some energetic and capable men and women were at work doing that developing. On December 1, 1899, this editorial statement endorsed the work of the settlers.

"Just a few miles west of St. Helens is a settlement of very prosperous people, the particular locality being known as Yankton. There they have a good school, a post office, general merchandise store, boarding house, and a sawmill, besides the logging and cordwood industry is carried on there to an extensive degree. The sawmill, which is owned and operated by Mr. H. O. Howard, gives employment to a number of men the year around, and though not having a great capacity, the product of the plant is good. Most of the lumber consumed in the neighborhood is manufactured at the Howard Mill, and is generally highly satisfactory. Mr. Howard puts in his own logs, at which work a number of men are kept constantly employed. The presence of the mill is a great convenience to the community and a source of profit to the owner.''

Farmers were so busy haying that the attendance at the Fourth of July festivities was not as large as had been anticipated. These settlers had a concept of New England thrift and a Puritan ethic: work came before even patriotic pleasure. Summer weather was a good time for Tom Holstein to have thirty acres of slashing done to get ready for a fall burning and clearing of more farm land. Tom, like many of the valley residents, was farmer, logger and mill man. R. H. Bailey and others in the spring were planting spuds and ''everyone was planting cabbage seeds.''

''The high price the farmer has received for his fruit, hops, hay, wheat, etc., encourages him to repair his barns, houses, fences . . .''

Joe Dupont bought a band of sheep from John Franz. John Franz in the early 1850s had settled on what became the Houlton-Pittsburg road just out of Houlton. The Franz hill still marks the area, near the Perry donation land claim. Franz was selling his sheep and cutting down on his land holdings. He and his wife Helena, ''for one dollar and love and affection'' deeded ten acres of their farm to their daughter Dora, who was just marrying Uther W. Clark. The real estate change is dated September 28, 1895. Mr. and Mrs. Uther Clark lived on that land the rest of their lives, raising a family of many sons. Uther Clark served the county in many different capacities, being at one crucial time of timber tax discussion the elected county assessor. John and Helena Franz also deeded ten acres of their farm to their

The Yankton community hall, built in 1902, in center; left, Yankton schoolhouse, built in 1909. The shed to the right sheltered horses driven to meetings.

daughter Clara on the same day. John Franz died in 1901 at the age of 65.

George Kelley of Houlton also bought a flock of 150 sheep to pasture on Bunker Hill. He paid from a dollar and a quarter to a dollar and a half each for them, and kicked himself for not buying them the year before when he could have bought them during the Cleveland slump at seventy-five cents a head. Joe Dupont sold his sheep in January, 1898, for two dollars a head. In November, 1898, one herd of three hundred sheep and cattle was driven out of the upper Nehalem valley down Milton creek going to the Portland slaughter houses.

The comments on fruit growing increased in the Columbia county area as Oregon fruit took its place in the world market. Mention was made of Medford yellow Newton apples being shipped to Germany, and the Columbia county possibilities were emphasized. "We frequently see parties from the Poland settlement and other ranchers from about Bunker Hill, packing fruit trees in to their clearings on ponies. Such enterprising citizens will be sure to vote for the plank road, and help to built it." This comment emphasizes two needs for the desirable development: planting orchards and improving roads. Comments on the promising potential are frequent: "The whole country drained by Milton creek has been fully tested, and the fact is brought out with distinctness that as a fruit growing section it is all right. Very few if any of the young prune trees have suffered from the freeze, and only once in ten years have fruit blossoms been injured by the cold spring rains."

In 1894 Columbia county grew 8,235 bushels of pears and apples. Most of these were from very young trees. Charles and Lawrence Tarbell, father and son, planted their fruit trees in the spring of 1893, yet in September, 1895, Charles wrote enthusiastically of his yield. "Our prunes are beginning to ripen and we find they make a most delicious sauce, shall have on one tree (5 years old) about two bushels." But the pears earned his warmest endorsement. "Wish you were here to help us eat our pears which are just

111

delicious. . . had to pick some to keep them from breaking down.'' He picked a pail of pears two weeks later, found that 26 pears weighed 16 pounds; ten ounces each pear, as he proudly proclaimed. He also picked a couple of pails of petite prunes, and found them good, though not as large as the Italian prunes.

Nickerson's diary in Vernonia mentions having strawberry shortcake June 13, 1891. Strawberries are mentioned in the Milton creek area throughout the decade, with Charles Tarbell ending the decade with the remark, ''We are just getting through the strawberry season having feasted on them the last few weeks.''

Other berries are mentioned as part of the attraction of the Milton creek land. Alice Brown in her first report in 1891 mentioned gooseberry, current, and blackberry bushes along with her list of fruit trees. Charles Tarbell, on noting the end of the strawberry season said, ''and now raspberries and wild blackberries are in order and are in abundance.''

Haying came in for frequent mention and the number of acres cleared and farmed increased year by year. Fences and barns were built and dairy herds were increased and improved. At Carico on upper Milton creek the farmers cooperated in improving their dairy stock, changing breeds to Holsteins, and Fred Briggs purchased several Jersey calves. The January, 1899, rumors of a possible creamery in Warren, with Portland money invested, proved to be true. The Warren ''skimming station'' was receiving one thousand pounds of milk a day by April. Yankton also was soon to have a ''skimming station,'' with local sponsorship. Lawrence Tarbell had a good hay crop and harvested about thirty tons from fifteen acres.

Charles Tarbell had a fine flock of thoroughbred Plymouth Rock hens and was offering setting eggs. The editor of the *Oregon Mist* wrote, ''Mr. Charles Tarbell . . . has succeeded in improving his Plymouth Rock hens. He has a male bird seven months old that weighs eight pounds, and pullets correspondingly large.''

Farming made some inroads into the Milton creek area in the years of McKinley prosperity, but timber harvesting was the principal activity and the source of income for most of the farmers. The reporter from Yankton wrote for the April 28, 1899, *Oregon Mist*: "The little farming done in this place has been promptly disposed of, and now all hands are ready for something else." The same column reported that four young men had come from Maine to work in Howard's mill. Howard's mill was turning out 200 railroad ties a day and Lawrence Tarbell, who considered himself a farmer, was driving the fine new team of horses which Howard had bought, trucking the ties to the Houlton railway station.

Howard had added a drying house for lumber to his mill in September, 1895. The next year Howard began making contracts to furnish railroad ties for the railroad company, the first being for 9,000 ties for the Northern Pacific company. He had at that time four teams hauling lumber or railroad ties. Soon he built a dam on Dart creek to facilitate log handling at his mill. In January, 1897, "Howard made a drive of railroad ties down Milton creek and through the Oregon Wood Company's flume to Houlton, with good success reported and much cheaper than transporting by wagon." In March it was reported that "H. O. Howard is rushing things at his mill. He will complete his tie contract about the 15th of April." He had been put behind by having to take an engine to Portland for repairs.

The December 23, 1898, *Oregon Mist* gave editorial approval to Howard as "the hustling proprietor of the Yankton sawmill" and reported an order from the Northern Pacific railroad for enough ties for two months' work at the mill for ten or twelve men. "Mr. Howard and his work has always given satisfaction. He is a thorough mill man." However snow collapsed the roof of the Howard mill in mid-January, halting work for a few days. Howard was resourceful at recovering from such problems and the mill was soon in full operation. In March Howard was in Kalama negotiating the purchase of a new engine. In September this large traction engine arrived. He purchased a fine draft horse named Rose and also a new lumber wagon. Herb

Howard had reason to believe as the century came to an end that he had contributed to the development of the potential resources of Milton creek. He was also to be heard from in the decade following. His work for Columbia county was far from finished.

While Howard's mill, its boarding house and related activities, was the most visible activity in Yankton during the McKinley years, it was far from being the only indication that the timber was being harvested. Cordwood cutting, logging, and shingle mills were also busily in process.

In the month of McKinley's election the conflict of interest among the users of Milton creek was commented on. "Milton creek loggers are losing a good opportunity for getting their logs out on this excellent natural flood which has been on for some time, on account of the Oregon Wood Company having so much cordwood in the creek." Mr. C. C. Moyer and his son Will were working in Stanwood's logging camp, though logging was at a standstill in December owing to a prolonged cold snap. Frank Brown's logging operations resumed in February after a winter shutdown. In mid-February the Milton creek loggers were busily engaged using the abundant water to get their logs out to market.

The creek was the avenue for logs to reach market, and as the new century opened there was an active market for logs. Multnomah county was cutting 200,000,000 feet of lumber a year while Columbia county was cutting 40,000,000 feet to be either second or third among the counties in the state in lumber production. Many of the Linnton, St. Johns and Portland mills used logs from Columbia county.

In January, 1900, the Milton creek loggers were happy with a run of a million feet of logs in one day. The logs brought the excellent price of five dollars per thousand. Milton creek was dammed in several places, the height of the main upper dam being raised in 1901 to increase the volume of water. To use the water avenue to market, crews of men also cleared the creek bed of brush and prepared it to take the logs. A successful drive of logs is described in December, 1901.

"Tuesday was a big day for Milton creek loggers as over a million feet of logs were driven out of that stream . . . The flood gates of the big dam near Yankton were raised early in the forenoon, and the tremendous volume of water and logs came with a rush and the drive was very successful. It is estimated that there were nearly two million feet of logs in the creek, but nearly one-third of them hung up in the creek near Crouse's place and another attempt will be necessary to get them to tide water."

The next week the writer could report success in the followup drive. "The big jam of logs which formed in Milton creek near Yankton last week was successfully broken last Tuesday. If good fortune favors, another attempt will land the logs at tide water."

Stanwood and Sherman Brothers paid off the mortgage on their company mill. "The company is prospering, with a good plant, good machinery, a good business." H. O. Howard closed out his Yankton mill in 1901, moving his machinery to Rainier, where he established a new mill with better access to timber. Early in 1900 the Stanwood and Sherman Mill was in operation higher up Milton creek than Howard had been. They had access to large stands of nearby timber. In January, 1901, Stanwood loaded a barge with ties and floated it down to the flume, then ran the ties through to the railroad. The railroad was using thousands of Milton creek ties.

As Christmas news in 1897 the *Mist* reported, "Wash Muckle and Thos. Holstein have formed a logging partnership and will put in several hundred thousand feet of logs this winter in Milton creek. The logging industry is receiving new life in all quarters. Saw logs advanced about $1.25 a thousand in the last year."

A year later, "Ed Stanwood, the Brinn boys, Wash Muckle, Tom Holstein and others who had logs in Milton creek are congratulating themselves on their good fortune in getting their logs to tide water, and are further congratulating themselves upon the good fortune in receiving $4.00 and $4.50 per thousand feet for them."

Stanwood and Brown had a raft of logs containing about 300,000 feet towed out of Scappoose bay, logs they had taken down from Milton creek.

The Oregon Wood Company had cordwood in the creek and it also used a flume into Houlton from two miles up the creek. Cordwood also was hauled on the road, about sixty cords a week being hauled from Bachelor Flat "when the roads are dry enough for hauling." A February 3, 1899, note read, "If there had been a wood famine in Portland as reported it is not the fault of Milton creek woodcutters. About 400 cords are now banked on Tedford and Milton creeks near J. N. Brinn's and more are ready to haul." The Oregon Wood Company ran 108 cords of wood out on May 20, 1899. In June Lawrence and Bert Tarbell were stacking the wood cut by the Oregon Wood Company's steam saw.

In August the wood business had practically ceased, owing to bad roads. The rainy weather (in August) was good for the farmer, bad for the wood men. In the September 1 *Oregon Mist* appeared the note: "One not familiar with our methods might be inclined to look upon the matter as a joke when told that it had been too rainy to harvest saw logs and cordwood." The paper carried regularly an advertisement by the Oregon Wood Company asking for 10 or more wood cutters. The discouraging factor for the wood cutters was that they had to wait 60 or 90 days for their pay.

Roads were an endless problem for the Milton creek activities. Howard had planked the road from his mill to the Houlton Station, but plank roads wear out, especially with heavy hauling. Some spots in the roads of the area were corduroyed, but mostly they were dirt roads, ungraded, up and down hills and around trees and stumps. The lumber and wood wagons rutted the roads until the expression "almost impassable" became a refrain. Mention is made of mud two and three feet deep on the roads. Hauling on the roads and running logs, cordwood, ties in the creek made weather conditions a determining factor.

Charles Tarbell commented in May, 1899, on the teamster activities in his family. Lawrence was driving a pair of horses for Howard, hauling railroad ties to the Houlton station. Bert had been driving an eight-oxen team hauling logs. Frank Brown had been down the river on the Coweeman at Kelso with a brother and cousin logging with eight oxen and five or six men. "We all have to keep busy to make ends meet . . . . Lawrence and Bert are having quite a struggle to get their places paid for and Frank and Alice have had it pretty hard." Driving horses or oxen paid well, but it was "a pretty hard job to tramp in the mud all day and manage six horses," especially in the wet climate. Roads were a never-ending problem.

The county cut twenty million shingles in 1894. Milton creek had at various times two or three shingle mills in operation. In April, 1898, shingle prices were rising. "Shingle mills are running again." Lumber prices, too, increased about $1.50 a thousand.

Milton creek had five logging operations, two shingle mills, and Howard's mill as the decade drew to a close. The area also had some signs of the price in human flesh paid by the workers.

Young men and older men bore scars and stubs of fingers as the badge of their employment. Certainly not all of the accidents happening in timber harvest in Milton creek were reported in the press, but enough were reported to indicate that the safety of workmen was not always the primary consideration.

One report in April, 1898, read, "John English smashed a finger at the Tuchenor mill last week and Lewis Orwig cut a fearful gash in his forearm Tuesday at the new mill of Orwig and Son. Will Dippold is just able to work again after a three week layoff from a saw cut on his arm. Several young men about here wear the badge of shingle mill operative in mutilated fingers and various scars about their hands."

David Pope was severely hurt at Brinn's logging camp on Milton creek. Leslie Bailey got his eye blown out in Howard's mill by a lubricator glass bursting. Sam Crosby got his fingers cut off in the mill. "The wounds are healing nicely." At Stanwood's mill J. R. Sherman caught his hand in a saw, losing a thumb and index finger and having the forefinger badly lacerated. One home accident attracted some attention. The two-and-a-half year old son of the R. B. Masons, little Earle Mason of Yankton, put his hand on a block where an older child was using a sharp hatchet. Three fingers were severed from his right hand, but Dr. Ross was able to save the partly severed little finger. This disfigured hand would not be by courtesy of a shingle mill.

Alonzo A. Smith on upper Milton creek lost a fine calf when it fell into Milton creek and drowned. Smith was an interesting character in the valley. He was widely known as farmer and logger, settling on Smith creek in 1890. He apparently got the itch to turn back to his earlier environment and get out of the Milton creek bottom mud and "almost impassable" roads, for the November 12, 1897, *Oregon Mist* carried the news, "Mr. A. A. Smith and family, who for a number of years have resided on Milton creek about seven miles from here [St. Helens], took their departure on Tuesday's train for Joplin, Missouri, where they will remain perhaps permanently. Mr. Smith will re-enter the zinc and lead mines at that place."

But Smith was not as pleased with Missouri as he had expected. He experienced a revival of Oregon interest. August 5, 1898: "Mr. A. A. Smith who about eight months ago left his Milton creek farm and logging camp and went to Joplin, Missouri, returned to this place on Thursday evening accompanied by his wife. Mr. Smith says the heat is something terrible there, and that the fruit crop is a total failure . . . Mr. Smith is satisfied with Oregon and says it is a better country for the laboring man than the East."

In March after his return to Milton creek he took work rafting logs on Scappoose bay for the loggers and moved his family to be near his work. That fall, too, he went down the river to work in the Brown brothers logging camp. But he returned to his farm on the upper creek bottom and lived there many years.

An important announcement for the community appeared in the December 18, 1896, *Oregon Mist.* "Charles Briggs of this place is building a store house in which he expects to put a small stock of goods." This sounds like a modest beginning, but Yankton was to have a general country store. Bert Tarbell followed this lead and opened a small store in Houlton in a building owned by H. O. Howard. Bert Tarbell's store venture did not endure, but that of Charles Briggs did. A May 12, 1899, editorial comment in the *Oregon Mist* was a hopeful forecast: "Fred Briggs was in town from Yankton Tuesday morning. C. H. Briggs and son are building up a nice merchandise business at Yankton, and their success is assured. They anticipate enlarging their storeroom in the near future when they will increase their stock to meet the demands of their fast growing trade."

The Yankton reporter for November confirmed the enlargement of both building and business. "C. H. Briggs has got nicely settled in his commodious new store. His success in the grocery business has warranted enlarging his quarters as well as his business. He carries a full line of flour, feed and choice family supplies." By that time the young Fred Briggs was clerk of the Yankton school district and "is kept busy between showers freighting for his father's store." He was not too busy for courting; he and May Burlingame, school teacher at Peris, were married on December 27, 1899.

In the last year of the century there were a number of public-spirited citizens along the way from Houlton to Vernonia. The school clerk at Yankton was Fred Briggs, and directors were J. N. "Nick" Brinn, Gordon Cloyd Barger and Frank Brown. At Peris Cornelius C. Moyer was clerk; Jesse Hendricks, John Wilwerding and D.R. Fowler were directors. At Valley William Miller was clerk; Frank Gliniecki, son of Valentine Gliniecki, Wilford D. Miller and Joseph Dupont were the directors.

The question of improving the road between Houlton and Vernonia was before the county commissioners and was being much discussed along the proposed route up Milton creek. Vernonia held a meeting in October, 1898, soliciting subscriptions of cash and volunteer labor to carry the project forward. Five hundred dollars worth of labor was pledged.

Herb Howard advocated a plank road. He offered to pay his ten-year tax in advance in plank supplied for the road. C.

L. Ayres of Peris had 300 acres of land. He said he would gladly pay the proposed 5 mill tax for ten years. He did not favor Howard's proposal. He said that corduroy from timber along the way should be used on the necessary places. However he was emphatically in favor of improving the road, however it was done. He said he saw an empty wagon deserted in mud holes out of which the owner apparently could not extricate it. Along such roads it was impossible for the farmer to get produce to market, difficult for him to do any essential shopping. Dirt roads did not hold up for heavy trucking in wet weather.

C. L. Ayres took the lead in securing signatures to a petition to the county commissioners to improve the road with money raised by a five mill tax to run ten years. The signers lived within three miles of the proposed road: C. L. Ayres, T. F. Stringfield, Abraham Crouse, Sardin Saulser, Richard H. Bailey, Charles H. Briggs, Charles Tarbell, W. L. Goheen, Joseph Dupont, Wilford D. Miller, William H. Miller, John King, Jesse Hendricks, D. R. Fowler, Solomon Rock, Frank Gliniecki, Frank Sobieski, Julius Floeter, A. F. Hardenbrook, Cornelius C. Moyer, Lizzie Faxon, Yankton postmistress, John W. Saxton, Christ Jensen, Herbert O. Howard, A. H. Tarbell, C. H. Webber, G. M. Brown, Harry Sherman, Fred Briggs, Val Wachowich, C. J. Wallis.

At Vernonia signers were Israel P. Spencer, E. A. Zillgit, John Pringle, Joseph Reed, H. D. VanBlaricom, U. M. Beeghley, W. E. Crissey, W. W. Allen, L. W. Van Dyke, John G. Pringle, Joe VanBlaricom, F. M. Parker, C. W. Mellinger, C. S. McNutt.

How the commissioners could fail to be impressed by this display of interest along the south county is not easy to understand until the rest of the county is considered. Clatskanie and Deer Island wanted roads into the Nehalem, and the roads down the Columbia were also very much in need of attention. In fact as the century ended, Columbia county needed roads. The county court at long last decided in January, 1900, to levy a road tax.

The Yankton correspondent to the *Oregon Mist* summed up the general community feeling of the early McKinley years: "Times are lively around Yankton, five logging camps being in operation. The McKinley prosperity wave struck Yankton shortly after the election."

As a sign of the future, the Northern Pacific built a steel railroad bridge over Milton creek, the first such bridge in the county.

As of February, 1900, Herb Howard was the sawmill man of Yankton. He had about 400,000 feet of excellent logs in his mill pond and was looking forward to a full run all summer. "He will cut a great deal of cedar this season for the Portland sash and door factories."

The Milton creek area had prospered under the benign sign of the good McKinley.

VIII: FOR THE FUN OF IT

*When I see how little the government has to do with
daily life, how self-helped and self-directed all families
are . . . I see what values America has.*

Emerson, "Civilization"

St. Helens was visited in August, 1891, by five Italians
and three bears, even a greater attraction than the more
common Italian with monkey and organ grinder. A crowd
gathered, such a group as the scattered populace of St.
Helens could muster, to watch the performing Italians and
dancing bears. "Anything to break the monotony" was the
remark of the commentator.

St. Helens had three saloons to help break the monotony.
It also received regular dockings of five river boats,
including the *Iralda*, which began serving the area down
river from Portland on May 10, 1891. But Muckles' mill
whistle sounded at five a.m.; a day's work was long and not
many people could sit around the stove in Dolman's general
store. An occasional Farmers' Alliance protestor-against-
the-establishment or the more common evangelist calling for
repentance and turning from evil ways or the rare magic
lantern show or even more rare Italian with bears was a
diversion from the mundane struggle for an existence.

However, the settlers found it possible to break the
routine of struggle with occasional social gatherings. These
festive frolics were most frequently dances, but a variety of
entertainment brought people together for social relaxation.
Leslie Bailey, the shingle mill man at Peris, gave a dancing
party. Alonzo Smith's new 18' by 24' house built by B. F.
Pope was warmed to occupancy by a dancing party. A little

sociable dance was given at Brinn and Holstein's camp on Saturday night, "a real enjoyable occasion." Herb Howard liked to dance and attended dancing parties at Peris and Deer Island as well as nearer home in Yankeetown. He even on occasion took his tame bear along. J. M. Burns invited neighbors to dance when his new house was ready. Jesse Hendricks and his two daughters Molly and Annie had dances in their Peris home. Dances were held in the Carico schoolhouse, one in July, 1892, being a grand success while one in August fizzled — only four men and three ladies showed up. Mr. and Mrs. Cushman at Carico hosted a dance party and the Bailey family enjoyed dances. Such musicians as were available along Milton creek were in great demand, especially Christ Jensen and his fiddle.

The lyceum was a popular method of bringing people together for sociability. The Nickerson diary indicates that the lyceum at Vernonia met regularly during the first years of the 1890s. It continued to meet with periodic breaks during the decade, even for some periods undertaking consecutive discussion of literary or historical subjects — Shakespeare, Burns, Tennyson and even Longfellow or the Revolutionary War and the father of our country.

The Yankeetown lyceum instituted the *Maineville Courier* as a weekly joke sheet aimed at airing wit at the expense of some local people. It must have been great fun for a while. But this lyceum more seriously came to debate such subjects as women's suffrage and the initiative idea. It even held a debate on the subject, "Resolved, that intemperance causes more misery than war." J. R. and Mrs. Sherman battled for the affirmative against E. S. Faxon, the teacher, and Henry Burnett, a team driver in Howard's mill and president of the lyceum. The occasion was also enlivened by singing, recitation and music.

Canaan varied the lyceum idea by organizing a Republican club which met frequently during 1892 and continued into later years.

Occasions for gathering in some home for festivity varied with the temperament of the host and the occasion. Deacon Charles Tarbell and his wife Nancy, as soon as they were settled in Yankeetown, invited friends in for a song party. Charles Tarbell liked to sing the familiar hymns of the Moody and Sankey vintage. He gave a more formal house-warming party as he moved into his newly built home. A late and abundant supper about eleven or twelve o'clock was standard for a dance or party. Dances were held in Houlton or St. Helens for one dollar or seventy-five cents, supper included. Warren even offered an oyster supper and dance for a dollar and a quarter. Abraham Crouse, like Charles Tarbell, invited guests for a sing party. Herbert A. Corliss varied it by giving a sing and popcorn party.

Mrs. William Ridley had a quilting party. The newly married Tina Gray Sweetland was there quilting. The Lawrence Tarbells gave a party for the sixteenth birthday of their daughter Iris. The D. R. Fowlers at Peris had an excellent party of games and music and an eleven o'clock supper. Peris also was the scene of a party put on by Kelso and Ridley.

The Duponts of Valley bought an organ for their home and invited twenty-five friends to help them celebrate the occasion. Muddy roads prevented the organ from arriving on time for the party; it arrived the day after. Friends and family gave the C. C. Moyers a party celebrating their twenty-fifth wedding anniversary.

The school entertainment was frequent; the county had between forty and fifty schools. The entertainment could be a program featuring "pieces," recitations, readings by pupils, with songs by pupils, parents or the teacher; or it might be a school picnic, a box social to raise money, or a special Christmas, Thanksgiving or even Valentine's party. The Carico valley school gave an entertainment which Herb Howard and his daughter Lizzie, a teenager, attended. The Yankton school put on a basket social to raise money for an organ, and raised $35.40. The Canaan ladies put on a box social benefit for their school. The Yankton school in February, 1897, put on a basket social to raise money to build a sidewalk from Yankton to St. Helens. In 1903, six years later, E. E. Hagen and Clyde Urie were the workmen building such a sidewalk.

Peris put on a special children's day program, inviting both Canaan and Yankton people. The Rev. Mr. Fairchild preached and a supper was provided; hot coffee was furnished.

The school social money-raising occasion was matched by the church money-raising social event. In July, 1892, the Evangelical ladies of Houlton raised $56.25 with a box lunch affair — a notable achievement. These same Evangelical ladies the next May gave a box lunch affair as a benefit for the minister, the Rev. Mr. Vincent. The amount raised for him is not mentioned. Some kind of "benefit" for a minister was a common way of meeting church budget problems. The Rev. Mr. Plowman received a barrel of miscellaneous clothing for his family from the Evangelical Women's Missionary Society in Williamsport, Pennsylvania. The Rev. Philbrook was the recipient of a donation party put on by Houlton ladies. Seventy-five people gave him $13 cash and a pile of provisions. Friends gave Martin Burlingame a shower, bringing in eight or nine dollars in cash and an equal amount in provisions. The Rev. R. B. Mason, the Methodist parson, was given a surprise benefit party at Yankton. The Houlton Methodist ladies put on a strawberry ice cream event to raise money for the Rev. Lew Davies, who served at Scappoose, St. Helens and Rainier early in the century. The Rainier ladies organized a fair and raised $40 toward building a Congregational church.

Columbia county has the longest border on the Columbia river of any county in the state. Thus it claimed a special interest in the river. When, on May 12, 1892, the centennial of the discovery of the river came around, the county was ready to blow whistles and wave banners. Two naval cruisers, the largest ships to enter the river up to that time, moved up the river from Astoria to Portland admidst the cheers and shouts of people along the banks. All the noise-making contraptions available were brought into play and spirits were as high as the noise was loud.

Another notable occasion was the opening of the railroad through to Astoria and Seaside in 1898. The first excursion train stopped at the various towns in the county to let local notables get aboard for the trip.

Excursions on the train began competing with excursions on the river and those who could afford either fare took picnic baskets and had a day or two of variety.

At the beginning of August, 1898, Clatskanie received the distinction of having an agent, "a very courteous gentleman named Smith," at the depot so that "we now buy our tickets instead of paying on the train." Thus the county developed.

Most of Columbia county was still, in the 1890s, undeveloped forest land, with abundant fish and wild life. Charley Brown and Charley Crouse went out from the Yankton school and in an hour were back with a deer on a day in September. Cougar were not plentiful, but they were present. A cougar killed John King's Jersey calf in 1899, and cougars were shot by hunters on occasion. One killed near the Charley Wallis place at Peris measured seven-and-a-half feet and stood three feet tall.

Bear were much more common in the inner county. Two black bears were shot at Valley in June, 1895. A large black bear was shot near the William Karth place at Valley in 1897. Also at Valley, Frank Gliniecki and John Wilwerding each shot bears in July, 1900. The real bear story of the county occurred in December, 1906, near Mist. Dave Kaye, a farmer, wounded a bear which then attacked him. He had to wrestle the bear for his life while he tried to get at his knife to finish the huge bear. He finally succeeded in dispatching the eight-foot four-inch, two hundred pound monster. The bear was exhibited at the Natal Grange. Kaye was patched up and put together again.

Camping out to fish or hunt, or "rusticating" on Bunker Hill or along one of the hundred streams in the county was a favorite break for many of the settlers, young or old. The young Tarbells and William Moyer went tramping in mud and rain over the divide to the Clatskanie and got nothing but wet clothes and colds for their trouble. The fortyish Alice Brown liked to go camping on Bunker Hill for weeks or even months, by herself, with her mother, or with her two younger sons and Iva Tarbell. She was an out-of-doors, fresh air addict. She also liked to walk and tramp over the hills, picking wild strawberries or wild blackberries in season.

In mid-August, 1893, an observer on Milton creek wrote, "A general exodus to the mountains has been in order for the past two weeks. A large number have gone into camp at Bunker Hill." The following week from Maineville appeared the note: "For the past three weeks the road through Maineville has been lined with crowded wagons going to and from the summer resorts on Bunker Hill."

Do not be misled by this language. The road "being lined" does not mean bumper to bumper traffic. It might mean four or five wagons a day for a few days. And "summer resorts" does not mean hotels or motels, inns or hostelries. There were no such rentable quarters on the hill — or between Houlton and Vernonia. What was available was a spring or a clear creek, a flat place for a tent and a tree for shade. This picture is made clearer by a note on September 7, 1894: "Bunker Hill seems to be a favorite camping ground this year, as almost daily teams are seen going by with a camping outfit, going to or coming from that place."

A sociable deer hunting, camping expedition on Bunker Hill was described in August, 1896. The camp site was up the Bunker Hill road past Eight Mile Spring — sometimes called Elkhorn Spring — where four men made a comfortable makeshift camp. Tents were set up and camp stoves, tables, seats, lounges, cupboards were set in place. After supper around a campfire the four talked and joked. The next day eight people joined the original four — women as well as men. "Bark Shanty Camp now began to assume a town-like appearance." More people came: ladies, girls, children. Evenings were spent in singing, recitations, conversation, games. The encampment lasted two weeks. Seven deer were killed.

A note in the *Oregon Mist* for August 16, 1901, contained an account of a camping excursion on the Nehalem. It is signed with the initials W.B.D. (probably W. B. Dillard, a young St. Helens lawyer). W.B.D. camped by a little brook two miles from Pittsburg, where he had available crawfish, trout, rabbits, blackberries; and the farmers of the sparsely settled area supplied what thick cream he could use.

Here in the "cooling shades of an ideal campground" he found delight in the Nehalem as it alternately plunged or glided through the dense forest. W.B.D. was a booster for the county. He wrote of the attractive little farms amidst the virgin woods of tall and thick forests. "A drive of ten miles brought us to the little village of Mist. Most of the people had good homes, large barns, good stock and an abundance of fruit, vegetables, hay and grain . . . . All of the roads would be greatly improved by the removal of timber left standing in the right of way which shuts out drying winds and sun and is an element of danger. We were incommoded on several occasions by dead timber fallen across the road."

The annual revival meetings at Vernonia gave many people particular incentives for following camp life for a few days and enjoying fellowship and song. Mrs. Herbert Corliss and Percie Briggs drove over from Maineville for a few days of the revival in August, 1893.

The inner county hills were productive of wild mountain blackberries, a delicacy fostered and developed by mother nature. Comments on the abundance of these berries and their desirability appeared from the earliest comments on the county. From the early 1890s people came from Portland and other places to camp out and pick blackberries. Settlers closer by could have a day's outing picking blackberries. N. A. Perry paid five cents a pound for picked blackberries in 1895 and the going price was fifty cents a gallon in 1904. By 1914 it was a dollar a gallon and blackberrying on Bunker Hill was still pursued. An observer from Pittsburg wrote in August, 1907: "Blackberries are ripe and plentiful. Campers are coming to our quiet nook and finding health and strength beside our rippling stream."

The Rev. Charles E. Philbrook and his son George camped out for a few days. The Warren school teacher, D. C. Allard, demonstrated his capacity to handle his very large classroom of students. He stood in the doorway of his school and shot a goose across Scappoose bay. He must have had his gun with him in the school. That was in February, 1900. He attended the teachers' institute that summer in Clatskanie and then camped out on Bunker Hill for a few days — undoubtedly with his gun — before the fall term began. The Warren people felt lucky to have him back. He kept the schoolroom in perfect order.

A very few of the more affluent people of St. Helens had their own land up on Bunker Hill for summer camping purposes. W. H. Dolman was one of the regular visitors to the big hill. He sold his St. Helens store in 1900 and had more time for "rustications." Throughout the 1890s he and his family used the Dolman camp. In 1900 U. S. Senator for Oregon, G. W. McBride, arrived from Portland for a couple of weeks' outing with the Dolman family on Bunker Hill. Mrs. Dolman was a sister of the senator and of Judge McBride. The Dolmans had spent much of the summer there, breaking camp and returning to St. Helens for the winter in September. This was not Senator McBride's first visit to the hill. In August, 1898, the *Oregon Mist* reported: "Senator McBride arrived down from Portland Tuesday evening on the *Shaver* and next day left for Bunker Hill, where he expects to remain two weeks rusticating and enjoying camp life. Other members of the family have been camped there for some time. The senator arrived in Portland from Washington about two weeks ago." Nor was the 1900 visit the last one for the senator. In 1904 he again was with the Dolmans on Bunker Hill.

When the Dolmans built a summer home is not clear, but in June, 1902, when they went to open their cabin for the summer they found it had been entered and their stove was missing. They moved from St. Helens to Portland but still came down to their summer home.

Dr. Edwin Ross did not build a home on Bunker Hill until 1907, and he was not looking merely for a summer cabin. Edwin Ross operated the St. Helens drug store from 1890, but he was also studying medicine in Portland. In 1894 he finished his medical coursework and became assistant resident surgeon in the Good Samaritan hospital. Toward the end of the decade he devoted his time to practice in the county while still running the drug store. He was a popular doctor, much in demand, and was called on to make trips miles out country roads at any time of day or night. In March, 1903, he married Matilda Muckle. In 1907 he bought Tom Holstein's land on Milton creek. The house on that farm had burned the previous summer while the Duponts were renting it. Dr. Ross built a comfortable farm home and set out to develop a farm with dairy cattle as well as a place where he could get away from his practice for occasional vacations. He entered exhibits in the Yankton Grange Fair of 1908 as evidence that he was entering the community. He was soon also serving on the road committee, being much interested in road improvement. Dr. Ross was a dedicated physician and an outstanding citizen, respected and admired by the hundreds whom he attended. In July, 1909, the W. B. Dillard family joined the Dr. Rosses in vacationing at the doctor's comfortable residence.

Hop picking was one way to combine camping with earning money. The Milton creek record doesn't say much about hop picking until about the mid 1890s. In 1894 some of the Peris people were talking about hop picking and a few of them really went. William Phole, leaving his wife to care for the farm, went to the hop fields as did Joe Dupont and Lester E. Bailey. The price paid to pickers was down in the general economic depression.

The fall of 1895 saw the real August parade from the Milton creek valley to the Willamette Valley hop fields begin. Joe Dupont went again and this time took his family. His neighbor William Miller left his tobacco field and farm and went along. The Mesdames Pope, Bailey and Luman left their families and went hop picking. More than twenty people got on one boat at St. Helens headed for the hop yards up the Willamette river, with Butteville the destination of many. They took along tents, bedding, cooking utensils for the annual fall migration. Charles Tarbell, who stayed home to attend to the farms, wrote that almost the entire neighborhood had gone up the valley. Iris Tarbell, who was pleased that she could earn nearly a dollar a day, mentioned that about fifty were in the hop yards from the Yankton area.

That the hop picking situation was causing some social problems is suggested by a note in the *Oregon Mist* from a Vernonia correspondent, August 26, 1898: "The mania for the hop fields has broken in upon the Nehalem and Rock creek people again. Nehalem and Rock creek valleys are nearly deserted. We are hoping there will be no compunctions of conscience, through their aiding in the liquor traffic. The timely advice given to parents in regard to unprotected girls in the hopyards we hope will be heeded. Too much watch and care cannot be given to both our boys and girls."

At the end of August, 1900, the roll of people going to the hopyards from the Vernonia area included:

Mr. and Mrs. Frank Tracy
Mrs. Israel Spencer and Robert
Claude Chamberlain
Sidney Malmsten
Miss Bertha Gillihan
Will Palmer
Ray Mills
Albert Baker
Mrs. E. E. Nickerson and daughter
S. G. Schoonover and wife
Elba Van Dyke
Mr. and Mrs. J. J. Block
Otto Cheldelin
Mr. and Mrs. S. D. Sheeley
Mrs. A. N. Early and family
Miss Vernie Sheeley
Miss Opal Spencer
S. B. Rose and family
James Emmons
Bert Hosford
John Smith and family
Mrs. R. Rogers and family
Miss Celia Van Dyke
Clarence Reed and son
Mr. & Mrs. W. P. Dereberry & family
George Sitts and daughter   *grandma Sitts*

One not named in this roll call was Mrs. Thomas Tucker. She was hop picking, her daughter was attending the teachers' institute, while Thomas Tucker kept the home fires burning too brightly. The house caught fire and burned to the ground. Tucker must have known where Mrs. Tucker kept her egg money for he saved the sewing machine with her twenty-five dollars in a drawer. The daughter had a fifty dollar gold piece in the house. It was found in the ashes. Insurance of $300 on the house helped cover that loss, but groceries and furnishings were lost.

People were finding other ways to enjoy the out-of-doors. In March, 1895, four venturesome young men bicycled to St. Helens from Portland. In June that year L. Crouse rode his newly purchased bicycle from Yankton to St. Helens. Lester Bailey received a new bike shipped from Chicago. The shortened word *bike* was used in the report. George Young of Yankton purchased a "bike and practices riding three or four hours a day in his log patch." If that isn't dedication!

By June, 1896, one observer said, "Bicyclists are becoming numerous!" In 1899 it was "the bicycle rage." Agitation for bicycle paths began and dreams of a bicycle path from St. Helens to Portland — especially from St. Helens to the county line — did not seem out of reach. It was said in May, 1899, that twenty or thirty bicycle owners by a small contribution from each could build a bicycle path from St. Helens to Warren to start the longer road. In June a call for a meeting of interested bicyclers was given publicity but only three or four appeared. It seems that it was seventy years after this talk of a bicycle path began before bicycle paths became a reality in Oregon.

Nim Baker of Warren, a 250 pound man, wrote humorously of his attempts to master the high wheeler. He fell off three consecutive times, the third time wrecking the wheel, but he vowed to get it repaired and master it.

Baseball was soon competing with bicycling for the interest of young sportsmen. The turn toward baseball in the county was not gradual; when it began it was a flood. Every little settlement had its team. Yankton played Warren on the Fourth of July; lodge teams played town teams. Riverboat excursions took fans with teams to games. Games were played in cow pastures with rocks for bases. Baseball became front page news in the *Oregon Mist*; it was a decade of baseball fever.

Various public events or celebrations were held throughout the county. School terms were usually closed with exercises to which the public was welcome, or by a general picnic for pupils and parents, or in some instances by combining picnics and exercises. Pupils were given opportunities to perform. The little program — with a supper included — at the Peris school in July, 1896, was typical. Alphonse Sauervein gave a welcoming address. Lester Bailey and Alphonse Sauervein presented a dialogue. Ida Wilwerding presented a recitation, "Who Spoke the Piece?" Cassie Wilwerding followed with a "moving" recitation and a dozen more mixed recitations, dialogues, and pieces followed, capped by a performance by the teacher herself, Miss Cheldelin of Vernonia, in "Miss Jones and the Burglar." Naturally, everyone had an enjoyable evening.

Churches were dedicated with public fanfare as were many other public or semi-public buildings. Christmas and Thanksgiving were publicly observed in most of the communities. At Valley the 1897 Thanksgiving observance was held at the C. L. Ayres farm where Mrs. Ayres provided a 7 o'clock dinner. The choir sang; Ada Schrader, Kissie Moyer, and Myrtle Ayres gave recitations. Mrs. Moyer, Willie Moyer and Myrtle Fowler gave readings, and the Rev. Mr. Fairchild spoke. The service closed with prayer and song.

The one holiday which received the most widespread and elaborate attention was the Fourth of July. It was still in the 1890s a day for celebration and rejoicing in memory of American Independence. In 1894 the little settlement still known as Maineville took notice of the day with a public program and picnic with free lemonade. The 1896 celebration was more elaborate. The citizens had cleared the picnic ground and instead of free lemonade had a refreshment stand offering candy, fruit, lemonade, ice cream. Certainly they had a program. They also had races for men and girls. "Come with a basket lunch and a hammock!"

The most elaborate Fourth of July celebration of the decade was held in 1898 while the war with Spain was on everyone's mind. Neer City celebrated with a patriotic program in the morning, a basket picnic, and in the afternoon a fat woman's race, an old man's race, a girl's race, a tug-of-war — all topped by an evening dance.

St. Helens invited the Ridgefield band to play for its celebration. In the St. Helens grove the band played, the Reverend G. G. Haley gave the appropriate prayers, (the Methodist minister was just starting to preach a series of sermons on Love, Courtship and Marriage, the first one being on the Rights of Women), the Rev. W. H. Iliff of Portland was the orator of the day. The Honorable Judson Weed read the Declaration of Independence. The afternoon was devoted to various games and amusements. The day was capped by a grand ball in the evening.

Clatskanie had an address of welcome by the mayor, band music, an oration by Judge Thomas McBride, vocal and more band music, and a grand ball in the evening.

Vernonia topped all of its competitors for the celebration of this memorable day. Vernonia was awakened at daylight by an anvil chorus. A program was held at the tabernacle at 10:30, a basket dinner at noon. The program continued at two p.m. with the Reverend A.E. Myers of Houlton the orator of the day. This part of the program was topped by an original poem read by the author, Mrs. Nellie S. Keasey, "The United States and its Development." Of course a dance came in the evening.

In July, 1902, Dr. Ross advertised that ice cream was available every Saturday at his pharmacy. Some notable events of that July were a camping outing on Scappoose creek, a crawfish feed/boat ride to Sauvie Island, and the seventy-fifth birthday celebration for the beloved pioneer doctor in Columbia county, Dr. Mrs. Elizabeth Perry.

Steamboat outings were very popular. Round trip tickets to Clatsop beach were advertised by 1895. The St. Helens picnic grounds offered an attractive place for groups wanting an outing; in July, 1892, fifty excursionists from Portland came on the *Cricket*. In June, 1893, the Pilots Association sponsored a picnic at the St. Helens grounds and fifteen hundred came from Portland for the occasion. In August another hundred Portland excursionists came. For the Fourth, crowds from Kelso and Castle Rock also used the picnic grounds. The Portland Unitarian Sunday school had a couple of summer outings there, coming down in the morning on one boat, returning to Portland in the evening on another. St. Helens school children on occasion took such boat rides to picnic in a Portland park.

Nelson Pinckney as early as 1893 was putting on magic lantern shows up Peris way and the photographer J. F. Ford, late in the decade, was showing magic lantern or stereoptican views of the nature scenery of the area. Both men were residents who obliged with programs. By 1900 a phonograph was played at public gatherings up Milton creek as a novelty.

Probably Clatskanie had the first motion picture theater in the county. By 1909 Mr. Kurtz had started a theater where "instructive moving picture entertainment affords an opportunity for passing a pleasant hour." With this opening Pearl White and Bill Hart were not far away. The magic lantern had begun to move. The author remembers going to the motion picture theater in Houlton in 1913, where a nickel would get a boy admission to the marvelous show.

Lillian Barger, granddaughter of Gordon C. and Annis Barger, was born in 1906. She wrote: "One of my very early memories is walking from our home to a social gathering on the lawn of the Lawrence Tarbell home. It was a warm summer evening and games were being played. All the ladies were dressed up pretty, with hair piled high on their heads, white highnecked blouses, long skirts, and high buttoned shoes. There was much laughter and singing. The Tarbell house was attractive, a neat white building, with mowed lawn, and a nice graveled road to the house that sat

Lawrence Tarbell in front of the home he built in 1909. The picture was taken on Memorial Day as he took flowers up to the cemetery. This is the home and yard remembered by Lillian Barger.

back from the road. It was across from the Briggs General Store and Post Office.'' Lawrence Tarbell built that house in the fall of 1909.

St. Helens had a roller skating rink in 1909 where the young people gathered. The Rev. Asa Sleeth, a brash young man who had served the St. Helens Methodist church for three years, attacked the skating rink as ''the gate to hell'' in a sermon. The editor of the *Oregon Mist*, E. H. Flagg, came to the defense of the rink and had a few words of wisdom for parents and religious leaders. The need was not for attacking a place of amusement but for sound moral education. Some seventeen-year-old youngsters would climb over a fence to get to the fires of hell. Parents needed to give them more basic moral instruction and be alert to their activities.

Year in and year out during the first decade of the century the grange was the most regular source for social occasions, giving regular monthly affairs for the community, hulled corn suppers, strawberry feeds, basket socials, taffy pulls — and always musical games and old-fashioned dancing. The meetings, discussions, programs and suppers were pleasant interludes to anticipate and they lingered as memories. One member wrote, "the meetings have done much toward making us acquainted with each other and have promoted a feeling of kindness and charity among us." The grange in many settlements became the principal outlet for community life. Goble Grange No. 329 handled the children's day observance in June, 1903, instead of church or school. The day was observed with a brass band, a program and the usual country dinner. Vernonia's Grange No. 305 in July, 1902, sponsored a children's day program with dinner for a hundred. In 1905 the Vernonia grange put on a Christmas celebration on December 15 with program, tree, entertainment and dinner. The members also worked that day in clearing the lots purchased as a building site. The Natal Grange No. 302 met in its new hall December 7, 1905, with a Christmas celebration. The grange master was N. O. Peterson, the lecturer (program chairman) Miss Ada Burriss, and the secretary Mrs. Nettie B. Peterson. The Natal grange was a thriving community organization. It sponsored the Fourth of July celebration. When it hosted the county Pomona Grange a hundred people attended, some coming twenty miles for the day's activities.

The Beaver Valley grange showed its mettle by debating the subject: "Resolved, that the farmer's wife contributes as much to the family prosperity as he does."

The Yankton grange hit upon an innovation and introduced an old-fashioned spelling match. It brought out a crowd and was repeated. These matches were held every two weeks for a time, Yankton even offering a broadside challenge to any community in the county. Mrs. Joe Sobieski was one of the champions, winning several evenings. School principal Ernest S. Faxon was also a winner. The social committee even tried an arithmetic contest, but it could not rival the spelling bee. The Scappoose grange also made use of the spelling contest entertainment.

Yankton had an organized chapter of the Order of the Red Men. As a part of the July Fourth celebration at Yankton in 1910 the Red Men paraded in their colorful uniforms on horseback. The lodge was organized in May, 1909, with twenty charter members. The group met twice a month in the grange hall, increasing in size to sixty members to begin 1913. Early in October they began their own building with Uther W. Clark as master builder, using volunteer labor. A box social was given in the new uncompleted hall with Jarvis Davis auctioneer; the auction brought in $257. (This was the first public notice of the coming to Milton creek country of the Jarvis Davis family from North Carolina.) January 10, 1914, the Red Men held a lodge meeting in their new hall. The building, across the road south from the Yankton school, became a popular dance hall. It was used as a grocery store and post office at the end of the 1920s and vanished during the 1940s, leaving not even traces of the foundation.

IX: LOGGING CHANGES

*" . . . it is not as ornaments that I value the noble trees of
this country, it is for their usefulness . . ."*
Judge Marmaduke in Cooper's *The Pioneers,* 1823

*The mission of men there seems to be, like so many busy
demons, to drive the forest all out of the country . . . as
soon as possible.*
Henry Thoreau, *The Maine Woods*

Herb Howard's residence was completely destroyed by
fire in August, 1901, while a crew of men was working in his
sawmill nearby. Few belongings were saved. Even the farm
orchard was damaged. Insurance partly covering the loss
was four hundred dollars.

Howard's mill had cut about all of the logs readily
available to it on Dart creek. Howard also was finding some
labor problems. With full employment available everywhere, laboring men were restless, continually going from
one place to another. Howard's wife Lucy came from the
Stehman area back of Rainier where still untouched timber
was available, so he bought timber land and moved his mill
operations to the new location. The machinery was installed
in the new place by the end of August.

Tom Holstein sold his logging operation on Milton creek,
and with J. N. Brinn started logging on the Coweeman river.
The Muckle Brothers also moved their logging operation
from Milton creek to the Coweeman. At the same time
Abraham Crouse and his sons were beginning logging along
Cox creek on Bunker Hill. Earl Saxon, born in 1888,

remembers logging with Abraham and Charley Crouse on Cox creek, using oxen to skid the logs to water. Earl Saxon's father settled on Bachelor Flat and had a herd of twenty-eight dairy cattle. His brother Sherman also farmed along Milton creek.

Several small family logging operations were carried forward along Milton creek and its tributaries on a month by month basis as water and sales were available. But the pace and scope of logging was changing over the county.

A bold headline in the *Oregon Mist*, May 25, 1900, read, "Reaping the Benefits of Republican Prosperity" over an article on the logging and sawmill situation on the lower Columbia where two thousand men were employed in camps, and logs brought six dollars a thousand. During the 1893-97 years only about two hundred men were able to find work in the camps, and logs in May, 1897, were $3 to $3.50 per thousand.

During these productive years, C. C. Masten of Skamokawa, Washington — who would soon make his appearance on Milton creek — was approaching logging operators to sound out the possibility for organizing to protect their interests against sawmill men. Thus in June, 1901, loggers along the lower Columbia agreed to close their camps for six weeks in July and August to reduce the supply of logs on hand by fifty million feet. "Persuant to an agreement of the Columbia River Loggers Association Muckle Brothers have closed down their Coweeman camps for 20 days. There will be very little activity in the logging business for the next two months."

In November, 1898, the *Oregon Mist* reported on a log run out of Milton creek: "The large jam of logs in Milton creek for several months was successfully broken and the logs are floating in Scappoose bay. The jam contained several million feet of choice logs which it was absolutely impossible to move without an immense head of water at the large dam, which resulted from the recent heavy rains. While this jam of logs hung up in the creek it has obstructed the wood company's cordwood movement. The wood company has over a thousand cords of wood waiting to go down their flume.

"The good results of this half day's work in opening the jam can hardly be estimated. The logs represent the labor of nearly every man living along Milton creek, as that industry is chief in that vicinity, and no logs had been run out of the creek in nearly two years. James Muckle says the jam contained about $12,000 worth of logs."

A million feet of logs was run down Milton creek one day in January, 1900, bringing five dollars a thousand.

A survey of the timber work up Milton creek appeared in the *Oregon Mist*, January 9, 1903. "While the present logging operations on Milton creek are carried on comparatively on a small scale and under low water conditions, the shipment of poles, shingle bolts and logs aggregate to a considerable amount during the year. Substantial dams placed at different locations along the creek enable logs to be moved readily when the flood gates are opened wide. Last Sunday the flood gates were turned loose, and thousands of Crouse's logs were set afloat down the stream.

"Dupont's shingle mill at Valley is running steadily and about 150,000 shingles are snugly packed awaiting shipment when the roads shall be in fit condition next spring. Duponts contemplate adding a sawmill next summer.

"Detrick and Keasy are running their Pittsburg sawmill steadily. This new mill has been running a couple of months.

"The East Fork Shingle Manufacturing Company of Pittsburg is running full time, producing 18,000 shingles Monday. Roddiman Brothers of Mist are running their saw and shingle mill full time.

"A half dozen other shingle and saw mills are operating near Mist and Deep creek."

Brinn and Stanwood built a new mill near Steward's corner on Milton creek in the summer of 1903 where much good timber was readily available. Brinn had the misfortune to fall in his mill, breaking a kneecap, and putting himself on crutches for a considerable time, but the mill was operative.

The Brinn and Stanwood mill in February, 1905, had a contract to cut 5,000 ties for shipment to California. The ties were driven down Milton creek to the wood flume and in that way floated to the dock in St. Helens for loading on a chartered vessel for San Francisco. Sherman Brothers mill at Yankton also had a large order for ties. Mitchell said, "The greater part of the timber in the hills will be taken out by means of small mills such as the Sherman and Stanwood mills." He was wrong in this prophecy, as the small mill was soon to be replaced by large mills. The Sherman Brothers mill closed out in October, 1906, to move to a new location in Bachelor Flat. In August, 1907, Brinn and Stanwood had orders on hand and were improving their plant with a slab conveyor system; and the Sherman Brothers in the new location also put in a slash conveyor system.

The Stanwood and Holstein mill in the spring of 1906 was running steadily, employing about thirty-five men. The two mills were keeping ten teams busy hauling lumber to the railroad at Houlton.

Herb Howard had his sawmill at Rainier in sufficiently successful operation for him to permit his son Calvin and Mr. Webber to assume responsibility for its work with him absent. In early 1903 he wanted to devote more time to his Yankton farm. That August the barkentine *Tam-O-Shanter* loaded a cargo of ties and lumber from Howard's Beaver valley mill at the Rainier wharf.

The July Fourth celebration must have been too much for young Calvin Howard. He was arrested, charged with assault upon Alexander Emerson, leading the writer for the *Oregon Mist* to say, "Howard is a hard working young man and if he would refrain from liquor would be a first class citizen."

The Howard mill cut about 20,000 feet of lumber a day. In July, 1906, it cut part of a cargo of lumber for Denmark. After five years of cutting at its site the mill had used the easily accessible timber. Howard still used oxen while other logging operators were using donkey engines. He moved his mill one mile to a new site where he considered that available timber would give him seven years, cutting. He

The Herb Howard sawmill at Yankton, early 1890s. Dart creek, in foreground, is dammed to provide the pond for log being hauled up at left. Large pile of sawdust in center comes from conveyor. Lumber at right, ready to haul to market. The present (1982) home is on site of house across from sawmill.

The Howard sawmill about 1900, Calvin Howard at right. The partly cut log is ready to be pulled by the cable-drawn carriage into the circular saws. Such saws limited the size of log which the mill could cut.

Herb Howard's sawmill about 1900. Howard is on the lumber pile beside the Miller twins, Herman and Norman. Norman later taught at Columbia Heights school during 1915-16. Calvin Howard stands behind the twins. Road conditions limited the size of the load of lumber.

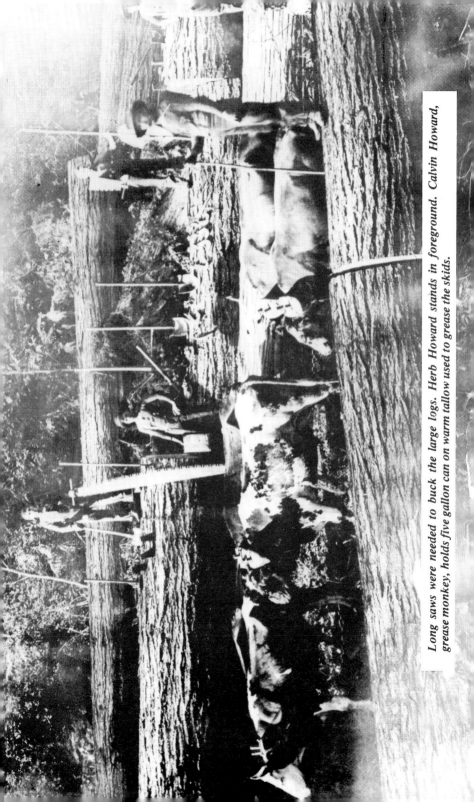

Long saws were needed to buck the large logs. Herb Howard stands in foreground. Calvin Howard, grease monkey, holds five gallon can on warm tallow used to grease the skids.

Bullwhacker Herb Howard with his six-yoke oxen team logging on Wikstrom land on McNulty creek. Ralph Hazen on left pinchboard; Everett Emerson on right board. Among those to extreme right are Mrs. Rudolph Kappler, Molly Howard holding son Harry, Lizzie Howard and Mrs. Wikstrom. All from Maine, men in background indicate size of a logging crew. The skid road is clearly evident in foreground.

... a with his goadstick, and oxen in action. Logs had to be hooked together with an eye to how ...ey would ride on the haul to water. Grease monkey Calvin Howard is also on the move.

The cigar-shaped ocean-going raft was developed under the leadership of Simon Benson in 1906 to transport logs between the Columbia river and Benson's San Diego mill. This raft is being assembled in a huge cradle, some 600 feet long, sixty feet wide and thirty feet deep, in the sloughs by the Clatskanie river.

Oregon Historical Society

Herb Howard with goad stick, three yoke of oxen hauling three large logs on the skid road. Young man seated on log holds a wood-headed maul used to set the dog chains in the logs. Iron sledges were not used on the dogs, as being too destructive on valuable equipment. Wood mauls could be easily replaced.

The ocean-going raft is here chained and ready for its ocean voyage. The cradle in which it was shaped is in the background. Tons of iron chains fastened the logs into a huge cigar shape. The completed raft contained about five million feet of logs.

Oregon Historical Society

The Maston locomotive, about 1907. Logs felled in woods are taken by train to water for transportation to mill or market.

built a log pond on a branch of Beaver creek and arranged his mill to have a capacity of 40,000 feet a day. He built a mile-long plank road to the county road over which to haul his lumber. "Mr. Howard is one of the solid men of the county and in a business way one of the men who is making Rainier a great lumber shipping point."

A logging railroad was started inland from Goble in 1901 and logging operations began on a large scale in the summer of 1902. The railroad brought out fifty rafts of logs in six months, the logging trains running late into the night to keep up with the logging operations. This was the Goble, Nehalem and Pacific Railway, the company having its sights on the Nehalem valley and then on to the coast. The Benson Logging Company in 1903 started building a logging railroad from Clatskanie toward the Nehalem valley. It was estimated that fall that thirty logging railroads, averaging four miles in length, were in operation on the lower Columbia. Benson had begun buying up timber land on Bunker Hill and the headwaters of the Nehalem and Clatskanie rivers by 1900.

The principal taxpayers in Columbia county, 1903, were timber holding companies. Little by little homesteads and small holdings of timber land were being consolidated into larger tracts. The railroad companies had their land subsidies, amounting to large acreage. The Northern Pacific Railroad Company paid taxes on its track and its ferry-boat *Tacoma* as well as its land, the tax bill being $6,486. The Astoria and Columbia Railroad Company paid $4,160. The Benson Logging Company was taxed $3,230; the O. and C. Railroad Company $1,569; Columbia Timber Company $1,342; Muckle Brothers $1,101; Yeon, Pelton Company $1,188; and the Oregon Wood Company $232. For 1906 the Benson tax was seven thousand dollars, the largest single amount in the county.

The S. Ban Lumber Company at Quincy was owned and operated by a Japanese. It was a thriving operation, selling about 10,000 cords of wood a year, 20,000 telephone poles, and doing a big shingle trade. S. Ban was also interested in farming, keeping a fine herd of registered Jersey cattle and Berkshire and Poland China hogs. Mr. Ban and his company built a Japanese style display for the Lewis and Clark Exposition.

The Oregon Lumber Company of Beaver creek, using a flume to get its lumber out, shipped about $250,000 worth of lumber a year.

Big timber deals were marks of the changing times. As early as February, 1900, the big deals had begun. Joseph Dubois of Pennsylvania bought 29,000 acres of timber land in the Nehalem valley, estimated to have 50,000 feet per acre. William Reid, a lumberman from Michigan, bought the Goble, Nehalem and Pacific Railway and its holdings for about $200,000. It had seven miles of railway track in from Goble and about 7,000 acres of timber land.

The Chapman Logging Company, building a railroad from Scappoose into the Nehalem valley, bought 11,344 acres of timber land in the Vernonia area.

The Muckles had timber on Cox creek and were said to own 4,000 acres of timber land. The county had about fifty sawmills in operation. The Western Cooperage Company was buying land on upper Milton creek at Trenholm. The company advertised for one hundred men to cut stave bolts.

The Clark and Wilson Lumber Company purchased 10,000 acres of timber land back of Goble for $800,000. The land was estimated to hold 400,000,000 feet of timber. This purchase included the Goble, Nehalem and Pacific Railway's ten miles of track and rolling stock, and gave William Reid a good profit on his investment.

This transaction took place in the spring of 1907 just as a money panic was hitting the country. The price of logs was dropping with oversupply and loggers' wages were rising too high for the comfort of the companies. Wages in the logging camps ranged from $3 to $6 a day. Boarding house grub was $4.50 a week. The logging companies made an abortive effort to improve their situation by closing camps for a time to reduce the supply of logs on the market and on starting up again expecting to reduce wages.

The camps resumed work in August with about 90 million feet of logs in the river, a reasonable amount to care for the demand by the mills. However, men were in short supply, full crews were scarce, and no attempt was made to lower wages. Board, however, was raised to $5 a week. Logs were bringing about $8.50 a thousand.

The C. C. Masten Company began building a railroad to their timber land on Bunker Hill in 1907. The Mastens were from Skamakawa, Washington, where they had logged for many years. The father, J. C. Masten, had been a county commissioner and his sons operated the logging company. They owned, as Alice Brown, mother-in-law of the youngest son, Delmer, said, "thousands of acres." This was Bunker Hill land with abundant trees waiting.

C. C. Masten built a fine home on the bluff overlooking the Columbia river in St. Helens as his logging operation got underway. This was to be such an operation as Milton creek had not known. Masten said that he had 20,000,000 feet of standing timber and that 100,000,000 more were readily available. The company employed one hundred or more men in the camp. It used five donkeys in the woods and three locomotives on the log haul.

Dr. James Withycombe of Oregon Agricultural College, on visiting the inner Columbia county, was impressed by the walls of forest on each side of the farmed land. The forest was immense wealth. A tree 250 to 300 feet tall, 175 feet to the first branches, would yield 10,000 feet of prime lumber. "Hundreds of thousands of such trees" were available in the inner county.

The active market in timber land and such public enthusiasm as that voiced by Dr. Withycombe led to an active discussion of property assessment in the county. In the fall of 1907 Benson Lumber Company holdings in the county were assessed at $1,700,000. The total county assessment was $16,788,640. The Northern Pacific Railway Company protested the assessment placed on its railroad holdings: $90,000 on the *Tacoma* and $65,000 per mile of roadbed. The court settled the dispute with a figure of $55,000 per mile for 1907 and $44,000 for 1908. The railroad's 1908 tax was $15,297.89.

The editor of the *Oregon Mist*, probably voicing sentiment generally expressed, urged the county to have a timber cruiser take readings on the timber in the county. Such a canvass was undertaken, but still the agitation and suspicion continued. Pleas were made for higher taxes on timber land to force a more rapid cutting of it. Thus the county could be opened more rapidly to settlement and agriculture.

In August, 1909, the editor's campaign focused on Simon Benson. Benson was reported to have said that his holdings in the county were worth four million dollars or more, while they were assessed at less than half the amount. Benson should be paying $10,000 more taxes than he is paying, the editor argued. Benson as a big speculator is not a benefactor to the county but a curse. The county could have many more small mills cutting the timber and hauling the products to cars and boats; therefore the timber could be cut out faster and more farming could be developed. Thus the editor approached the problem.

Benson developed the huge cigar-shaped rafts for towing logs to San Diego, where he built a large mill. In this way he took the logs and the mill to the market instead of shipping the lumber to the market.

That Columbia county had a vast resource in its twenty billion feet of prime timber was clearly understood, but it was also regarded as a county with rich agricultural potential. America was still agrarian and settling on one's own farm land was still the ideal. How to cope with the problem of getting wood products out of forests, getting the products to market, giving labor a wage to live on and "developing the county" defied reason and confused hopeful expectation.

A cry of despair came from Pittsburg in November, 1910. William Elliott was moving to Olympia. He sold his place to the Pearson timber interests "who own pretty near the whole of the Pittsburg neighborhood. The Nehalem population has decreased rapidly during the past few years . . . The whole country is a sad tale of the control of the timber land speculators For one house that is inhabited there are four that are not, settlers having sold their land and left." The writer said that eventually the railroad would come into the valley and the timber could be harvested.

Simon Benson went to work as a bullwhacker on Tide creek out from Deer Island about 1880, just after Herb Howard first landed in Rainier. With the first money earned there he bought 160 acres of timber land at $5 an acre, the land containing about six million feet of timber. He logged his own land with his own oxen. He sold out after three years for six thousand dollars, returning to logging on Beaver creek near Clatskanie after a lapse of five years. From this 1888 start he developed his business rapidly. Working on the Washington side of the river at Cathlamet in 1891 he built the first logging railroad on the lower river. The Benson Logging and Lumber Company dates from 1895. Simon Benson towed the first of his famous oceangoing rafts out of the Clatskanie river to San Diego in 1906. He sold the Columbia county holdings that he had built up in June, 1911, for about five million dollars. This sale involved his rafting appliances, a sawmill at Clatskanie, 15,000 acres of land with about 800,000,000 board feet of timber.

The C. C. Masten Company, over the economically troubled fall of 1907, was in full operation, hauling about 80,000 feet of logs a day to Scappoose bay. They got a special order for the Eastern and Western Lumber Company of Portland, an example of high-balling in the timber industry. It was a rush order for a ship loading in Portland for Australia. The Mastens got out four sixty-foot logs and four seventy-foot logs to be sawed into 16 x 16 and 20 x 20 squares. They also got out logs for two 20 x 20 sticks a hundred feet long. The time from tree to shipside was three days. The logs were ordered on Saturday, felled in the woods, hauled on the railroad to water, towed to the mill in Portland, sawed in the mill and were on the boat on Monday bound for Australia.

Logging in the Milton creek watershed had been done by small operations where the man managing the operation and employing helpers worked beside his employees. The Brinns, Stanwoods, Holstein, Howard, Crouse, Smith and the Tarbells and Browns were all settlers in the area, mostly logging their own small holdings. A small crew of six or eight men worked with the employer-boss. Many of the workmen were farmer neighbors of the operator of the small camp. The Masten family of brothers who came to Yankton to begin logging operations in 1907 do not stretch that concept of the small operator working with his men very much. Mr. and Mrs. Roland Masten were living in one of the new camp homes by March, 1907.

The Mastens built the most permanent camp Milton creek had known, with homes for the married employees and bunkhouse and cookshack for the single loggers. The family of Alice Brown came to be closely associated with the Masten camp operation, and through the Tarbell letters the development of the camp can be followed in some detail. The Mastens first came to the community as timber cruisers or scalers to look over their timber land before the railroad and camp were built. As the railroad was built into the timber camp, homes were built for the married brothers. Delmer was the youngest, twenty-three and unmarried. He soon began taking notice of sixteen-year-old Beth Brown, whom he married in June, 1909. Long before the marriage, Beth's three older brothers, Perley, Charlie and Eber, were working in the Masten camp. Delmer was engineer on the logging train and Eber was fireman. The track ran across a corner of the Brown farm and Alice daily could hear the whistle of the train as it passed loaded down the creek or empty on the return.

The young prospective bride tells of what she sees just ahead. "Delmer is seven years older than I am and very dark complexioned with brown eyes, we have told you about Mastens big logging concern a mile from here . . . where our three big boys work. Delmer's brother is head manager of that and Delmer is the engineer on their locomotive. We will live at the camp for a while in a little house of our own, as many of the other families do, and I wish you could see the pretty little homes they have, just as nice as anyone would have in town. The camp has the reputation of being the neatest and best kept camp on the Columbia river and it certainly is nice. One of Delmer's brothers lives there with his wife and we are great friends."

Eber Brown, fireman on the Masten logging locomotive, gave this photograph about 1910 to Cassilda Wilwerding, whom he was courting.

Alice Brown's comment was, "The Mastens are not rich, only busy men, handling rather large interests." Effie Fitzgerald, who came to teach the Yankton school, married Charlie Brown and the two newlywed couples moved into adjoining houses at the camp, next to Delmer's brother's house. Thus the three related families were immediately together at the camp. The two young brides had lace curtains, comfortable furnishings, and Beth soon had a piano. A telephone — a great convenience to all — was installed at the new camp.

Charles Tarbell went to the camp to visit his granddaughters, but aside from having his picture taken by the creek holding his great-grandson, his interest was centered in the wonder of the logging operation. He rode out with the engineer on the train loaded with seven cars, with six to nine trees on each car, one about 100 feet in length, "twas quite a sight . . . I asked the engineer about how many thousand he had on and he estimated it at 45,000. They are worth 10 dollars per thousand at the river, so you see he had about $450 worth and they make three trips a day. Their expenses including stumpage is about $400 a day so you see they are making some money."

Aside from the money question Charles was more deeply interested in the handling of the logs by machinery. He devoted a page to describing the operation of assembling and loading the logs on the cars: ". . . up goes the log ten feet in the air and then it gets rightly balanced over the cars is let down on to them as easily as one would lay down a small stick of wood."

The logging oxen had a decade earlier given way to the horse and the donkey engine. Now the water of Milton creek was losing its importance in getting logs to market. When the last log run down Milton creek was made is not clear, but it must have been not long after the whistle of the Masten locomotive began to sound up and down the valley. The Stanwood mill was quick to take advantage of the new railroad to get its lumber hauled to market. In the fall of 1907, within three months of the opening of the railroad to log hauling, the Stanwood mill planked the road the mile from the schoolhouse to the railroad crossing, hauling their lumber there to be taken to Houlton for reshipment. Still, in 1907, planks were put down instead of crushed rock to keep the lumber-trucking wheels from miring too deep in the mud.

The Christmas of 1907 was not an easy one for the employees of the Milton creek valley. The money panic of the east was affecting various operations. The St. Helens quarries were down and the Houlton Western Cooperage plant was silent. The *Oregon Mist* editor commented on January 17, 1908: "The whistle of the Western Cooperage Company plant at Houlton made pleasant music to those it called back to work last Wednesday. The enforced idleness has been anything but pleasant. It is hoped that the quarries will soon be running."

Ten days later the quarries were expected to resume operations. "The quarry is and probably always will be the chief industry of St. Helens," wrote the editor. That was not very good prophecy. The quarry did resume operation and it expanded its operation with an "immense steam shovel" which, over July, it transported from the railroad to the quarry. The machine was expected to do the work of about a hundred men. It cost ten thousand dollars and the freight charge on it from the east was thirteen hundred dollars. The method of moving it the two miles to the quarry was to lay 200 feet of track, move the machine on it, take up the track behind it and put it down ahead for another move. The operation required about fifty such moves.

The year had not yet passed before the editor's remark on the chief industry was to be brought in question. Timber was to be king for a time yet. The October 23, 1908, *Oregon Mist* carried news of importance: "The long-hoped for sawmill at St. Helens is at last to be built. Charles R. McCormick Company have purchased the Muckle site. The mill will have a capacity of 100,000 feet in ten hours. The work of construction will begin in ninety days. With the quarry and the new mill St. Helens will be one of the busiest and best towns in Oregon." The Masten railroad was making possible a steady supply of logs for a big mill at the mouth of

The St. Helens "Big Mill," about 1917 as seen from the county courthouse. The four-masted sailing vessel is loading lumber at the mill dock. The point of Sauvie Island is in the background.

Scappoose bay. Through the winter news of the company and the proposed new mill was front page copy. The company bought almost a mile of waterfront from James and Charles Muckle. The company had five steamships to carry its own lumber to California. It was expected that the mill would be completed by July 1, 1909, at a cost of about $200,000, to give employment to about two hundred men. It wasn't in operation by July, but it was in October.

The *Mist* editor by the new year was ecstatic over the St. Helens development. "The city of St. Helens is to be one of the busiest small communities in the state this season. The streets of Portland will take four million basalt blocks, bringing wages of $120,000. The two quarries have a large force of men producing crushed rock. The big mill has a payroll of $400 a day." The editor saw salmon fishing as producing about $60,000, a new water system about $40,000, and in addition all of the home-building and minor industries of the community. "Altogether it looks very good to the *Mist* man and it is going to keep on getting better."

The McCormick company had by June, 1909, persuaded the city council of its responsibility. The council granted it a twenty-five year franchise for a city light system. St. Helens was to get electricity. By the end of that year the McCormick Company was also promising to bring wireless telegraphy to the city.

The *Oregon Mist* for December 24, 1909, reported that arrangements for the wireless were made. The 200-foot pole would be the longest in use. "The station will receive wireless messages from all parts of the world." E. A. Crouse had the contract to build the two small houses which would receive messages from ships all along the coast, keeping track of the McCormick ships, and news of general interest. The company proposed to have news messages posted on a bulletin board for public reading, "elections, baseball scores, prize fights" and other news of importance. "This is certainly a great event for St. Helens."

If developing industry and an increased payroll were "keeping on getting better," the *Oregon Mist* man was entirely right in his hopeful attitude. Even the elderly

Charles Tarbell felt the pride in the expanding and developing commerce: "I was over to the camp last week and went with Eber (who by the way is running the engine that hauls the logs to the river) to the landing. They are just finishing a large sawmill right beside his landing that will require three large boilers to run it. [They] have put in a creosote plant that holds ½ a big liner full of creosote and have a tank nearly as large to hold the coal oil they run their engines with hauling logs. Then there is a shipyard just a little way across from the landing with two large boats nearly ready to launch. So altogether it was worth the trip to see." This was in 1912, showing the continuing expansion of the timber industry at the mouth of Milton creek. Up Yankton way the increased commerce was bringing expansion, too. In 1913, Charles wrote that "things are moving quite lively with us this summer. The lumber concern that the boys are working for are building some five miles of railroad extending their line further into the woods. [They] have about a hundred men to work on it and it looks like they might lumber here some years yet. About six miles west of us (at Pittsburg) a new stave factory has just commenced operations that turns out four two-horse loads per day that go past us to the dryhouse near the station."

X: THE CITIES DEVELOP

Without these [craftsmen] shall not a city be inhabited,

And men shall not sojourn nor walk up and down therein.

. . . they maintain the fabric of the world.
Ecclesiasticus XXXVIII

When John Dibblee landed in Rainier in February, 1869, he found only four buildings owned by white men. A small settlement of flathead Indians was nearby. The buildings were a sawmill, a general store, and the residences of Dean Blanchard, who built and ran the sawmill, and Joseph Silva. Dean Blanchard had been active in St. Helens many years before he first bought land in Rainier in 1869. Dibblee was born in New Brunswick in 1837, married Sarah Blanchard in 1862, and came to Columbia county where he lived until his death in 1910. The Rainier voting precinct showed a population of 116 people in 1870; 1,969 in 1910.

During these forty years Dibblee played a prominent part in the development of the area. He was one of Rainier's first councilmen, president of the Board of Water Commissioners, vice-president of the State Bank of Rainier, owner and developer of the Rainier Independent Telephone Company, which at the time of his death had one hundred subscribers. He also had developed and owned the biggest stock ranch in the county.

Rainier was the first city in the county to incorporate, November 25, 1885. It had sawmills and saloons before it

The town of Rainier, looking east. Mount St. Helens in background, about 1910-12.

had a school house and a church. The 1890 census showed the Rainier precinct as having 681 persons, the city of Rainier 238. The school district needed a second school teacher and had to build a new two room school in 1891. That September Rainier was also building a Masonic hall and a city hall. New residences were being built.

Rainier's most active period of development came in the five years before 1910, seeing the population increase from five hundred to two thousand. The timber harvest was in the bonanza days for the small logging camps and mills, before the big operators took over. In 1909 the Rainier area had eighteen shingle and sawmills and various other wood factories, such as sash and door plants. This town was the center of active logging operations, the whole timber complex giving the town a payroll of over fifty thousand dollars a month. The saloons helped keep the money from bulging the pockets of these loggers and mill workers. The churches and a few anti-saloon family people fought a running and losing battle to keep the saloon-keepers within decent bounds.

The alcohol or saloon issue generated about as much public emotion as the roads issue. The years of the most pronounced growth for Rainier were years of heated conflict over the liquor question, not only in Rainier but also in the county and state. Rainier seemed to be a focal point for conflict in the county. In the summer election of 1904 the prohibition party organized the county and put up candidates for local office. Lawrence Tarbell of Yankton was the most active and most successful of the candidates, though he, like the others, ran far behind the two major parties in votes. The issue was not the candidates but the wet or dry vote for the county and the question of local option. Various towns changed from wet to dry or dry to wet in the state and in the county. The law and order people lost the 1904 election to the "saloon element" in the county by only four votes.

In the spring of 1906, as the election issue heated up, a hired thug from Portland severely beat up the Rainier anti-saloon league spokesman, a Mr. Fisher. Threats of violence were made against the active Methodist minister, the Reverend H. G. Kemp, threats that the thug would return and "get him." The assailant escaped across the river and eluded arrest, even boasting that he had been hired by the saloon-keepers of Rainier. The authorities, prodded to action by the public clamor, charged the five saloon-keepers with violating the law regarding closing hours, fining them each ten dollars.

The editor of the *Oregon Mist* wrote : "The anti-saloon league of Rainier is asking for nothing except enforcement of the law and if the saloons cannot acquiesce in the demand the sooner they are put out of business the better." The Pomona Grange passed a resolution condemning the brutal attack upon Fisher.

The Yankton W.C.T.U. met every month to encourage interest. The editor of the *Oregon Mist* took a firm stand. Under the headings, "The Fight Is On," he wrote: "There is neither health nor wealth, true friendship nor pure love [in whiskey] . . . The amount of good it has done the world is a negligible quantity, but no one doubts or denies the immense evil. It's up to you, don't dodge."

The 1908 June election also involved the wet vs. dry issue. Thirteen formerly wet counties in the state voted dry, but Columbia county by a close sixty-four vote margin continued wet. St. Helens and Houlton both voted wet. Immediately five applications for saloon licenses for Houlton were filed. The license fee was $400. In 1913 Clatskanie voted dry by forty-nine votes.

Rainier could boast in 1909 of having a few gravel streets, electric lights, a water system, a number of religious denominations holding more or less regular services, and six general merchandise establishments serving the community.

In the spring of 1909, William Kennedy, a Hood River fruit grower, sold his fourteen acre apple orchard in Hood River for $23,000 and bought a Rainier farm. He expected to clear it and plant a hundred acre orchard. He also had a hundred goats and a hundred head of cattle. The Rainier Boosters Club publicized this move, advertising that Hood

River apple growers were investing extensively in land near Rainier. They boasted that the Rainier section contained the finest farm land for stock, dairying, fruit and diversified farming in the United States. "It is no uncommon thing for the first crop of potatoes on a patch of land to pay for not only the cost but the clearing of the land as well." Farming was still in its infancy with thousands of acres of rich logged-over land waiting for stump clearing and the plow.

The large family of children of Mr. and Mrs. James Muckle, Sr., of Montreal, Canada, settled in Columbia county in the 1870s, getting footholds in various parts of the county. The brothers were Robert, James, Charles, Washington and William; the sisters Mrs. Dan J. Switzer, Mrs. Richard Cox and Mrs. Jacob George. Mrs. James Muckle, Sr. died October 13, 1892, at St. Helens.

William J. Muckle established a mercantile business in Rainier and was, over his lifetime, one of the prominent citizens there. James Muckle located in St. Helens in 1874, buying with his brother Charles a sawmill on the Columbia river waterfront. James Dart, who built the mill in 1866, remained for a time as mill superintendent. The Muckles brought their brother-in-law, Jacob George, to St. Helens to run their mill.

The *Oregon Mist* began publication with Volume 1 in 1883, William Glendye, editor and publisher. Number 2 of that volume, February 2, 1883, contained an advertisement on the front page for the James and Charles Muckle mill and general merchandise store. The Muckle mill continued to operate until it was burned in 1904, and was not rebuilt. The Muckle store continued to thrive. In 1910 the Muckles built a brick building which became a landmark in the city. From 1886, W. H. Dolman operated a general merchandise store in St. Helens in competition with the Muckles.

The Muckle operations in the St. Helens area were varied and changing over the years. James and Charles Muckle opened a hardware store in 1875. It was later sold to William Muckle, the Rainier merchant, and Washington Muckle, who continued to operate it.

Washington Muckle's development was principally in logging, both on Milton creek and on the Coweeman, out from Kelso, but he also developed a ranch at Warren. The Muckle family, largely centered around St. Helens, left a legacy of active business development. In 1910, Charles Muckle built one of the most imposing residences in the county, costing about ten thousand dollars. The builder was J. H. Griffis.

St. Helens, at the close of the first decade of the new century, like Rainier, had a few crushed rock streets, electric lights, a water system, a few telephones, a good school building, and a variety of business houses. It had more churches — three — than Rainier and fewer saloons.

The local rock quarry in December, 1910, employed twenty-three blockmakers who earned from five to seven dollars a day, working at piece work, and seventeen laborers receiving two-fifty or three dollars a day. The quarry had work ahead for all winter, "if weather permits." St. Helens quarries had furnished paving and building blocks for forty years, though that work for the paving industry was soon to end.

The city had good hotels — the three story St. Helens Hotel had eighty rooms — the county courthouse and county offices, and a beautiful site. Moreover, St. Helens was just at the beginning of its period of most rapid growth and business and industrial expansion while Rainier had reached its apex.

The 1870 census figure for the Union precinct (St. Helens) was 144 persons. The area grew to 496 by 1880 and 812 by 1890. Of these 812 persons in the voting precinct — which took in the whole Milton creek and Gillton areas — only 220 lived in St. Helens. The city was incorporated February 25, 1889. The area around St. Helens continued to grow faster than the town itself. In 1900, the Union precinct contained 908 persons, St. Helens city had 258; but the Warren precinct had been taken out of the Union precinct, with its 295 persons. Union precinct doubled its population during the first decade of the new century, but St. Helens tripled its population. In 1910, Houlton had 347 persons, St. Helens 742.

During the years of Rainier's most rapid expansion, Houlton had grown along with the county seat town. Houlton was on the railroad. G. D. Gilson built a sixteen room hotel, the Houlton House, near the railway station and a livery stable adjacent to the hotel.

The Western Cooperage Company began buying up timber tracts in the upper Milton Creek area in 1903 and continued buying over the next four years. The company built in Houlton one of the best cooperage plants in the West. The company had a display of barrels at the Lewis and Clark Exposition in Portland piled thirty feet high, from a "great big fat fellow with a storage capacity for a winter's sauerkraut for a German hotel to a little barrel on top the size of a pickle." The Western Cooperage plant was the largest employer on Milton Creek, with its bolt camp at Trenholm, its crews running bolts on the creek to the plant in Houlton. The bolts were blocks of wood from which barrel staves were sawed in the cooperage.

The summer of 1904 was an economically slow one. Harry Oliver had opened a mercantile store in Houlton that spring with expectations of building a thriving trade, but the cooperage payroll was at a standstill. Houlton had just started its own newspaper in competition with the *Oregon Mist* and the affairs of the developing community can be followed for a couple of years through the pages of the *Columbia Register*, edited and published by R. H. Mitchell, a hustling editor with a caustic pen. His opening statement read, "The policies of the paper will favor good government as opposed to Republican misrule." He succeeded, whatever issues he sponsored in his running battle against the *Oregon Mist*, in showing Houlton as a growing town.

The Oregon Wood Company loaded a schooner with 400 cords of wood for the California market and the new Western Cooperage Company shipped two carloads of barrel staves to California. Over the summer the plant was shut down for lack of bolts while the water was low in the creek. In

Harry Orville Oliver,
the Houlton merchant, about 1904.

September the company had a crew of men clearing Milton creek and removing obstructions. They also had a dam built so that at appropriate times they could flush their bolts down the stream. "In about a week or ten days," the report was, "the work of clearing the creek will be finished and the bolt cutters will commence operation as soon as the fall rains set in. The cooperage plant will be started as soon as bolts can be run down the creek. Houlton people will welcome the sound of the factory whistle with joy."

The Frank Brown farm house at Yankton, a large frame building having twelve rooms, was used as a kind of wayside inn for bolt cutters and men working the river. Charles Tarbell wrote, "Frank called on us in the afternoon [Thanksgiving day]. He had eleven stream drivers stop with him last night and will have as many occasionally through the winter. They are running out bolts for the stave factory. They have some 50 men in the woods and Frank is supplying them with meat and butter so we have a market for all we can raise and make."

The Western Cooperage Company was also offering to remake the face of Houlton. The *Columbia Register*, October 21, 1904, extended the offer. "The Western Cooperage Company have their electric plant installed, and after testing it, find that it is possible to serve the town of Houlton with one hundred lights. If the people of the town desire the lights, some understanding should be had soon, so that the company can wire the town and be all ready to serve the town as soon as their plant is started up for the winter."

An editorial in the November 4, 1904, *Columbia Register* gave a survey of the town. Discount some of the superlatives and it is a good thumbnail sketch of this little unincorporated village.

". . . A short time ago the trains went whistling through as though no town existed anywhere near Houlton. But today it is different. Six trains a day stop at Houlton for passengers going to and from this station. Large consignments of shingles, lumber and farm products are shipped from Houlton. Houlton post office is the distributing office for more than half the territory of Columbia county . . .

"Houlton has the largest and best cooperage plant on the Pacific Coast — which turns out barrel staves by the million . . . . Houlton has two blacksmith shops . . . There are three general stores where large stocks of goods are kept. A barbershop, two hotels, and a restaurant. Two saloons, a jeweler shop, a shoemaker shop, and a newspaper office. It has an opera house in which some of the finest plays are put on during the winter season. A fine church edifice where public worship is held regularly. A fine graded school . . . All

Houlton Main Street, about 1909

174

Houlton Depot, about 1911

in all Houlton has about everything usually sought in a first class unincorporated town.''

Mitchell proceeded to express his judgement on what was lacking: ''Houlton needs many things. A box factory A shingle mill. An iron foundry. A woolen mill. A creamery. And about 2,000 good sturdy business men — men who can farm, grubbed stumps, built houses, plant gardens . . .''

In the line of being a businessman no one else earned the kind of accolades and attention which Mitchell gave to Harry Oliver and his mercantile business. The May 27th newspaper reported: ''Oliver the merchant has just added a fine new one horse wagon to his business equipment.'' In October the editor noted: ''H.O. Oliver has purchased the building where he is conducting business and is making some substantial and needed improvements. He has added a new barn and has arranged to carry a full stock of feed, including hay and grain. We are pleased to note that trade is improving in his line.''

In November H. O. Oliver was commended for laying a new sidewalk from his store to the blacksmith shop. In December the editor noted with both wit and approval: ''H. O. Oliver is putting on a little metropolitan airs. A new street light at the corner of his store is the latest.'' In the January 6, 1905, issue the editor gave a genuine endorsement of the Oliver store, even though three general merchandise stores in Houlton advertised in the *Columbia Register*: ''H. O. Oliver has one of the best up-to-date country stores in Columbia county, where you can find anything from a needle to a crowbar or from a wheelbarrow to a threshing machine. He has only been in business a short time but his trade is increasing and his stock growing.''

The growing Houlton was short of housing and Harry Oliver built a new home for his family of four children, getting them out of the apartment in the store building. The Oliver family lived in the new house only a few weeks, but the house in 1982 still stood.

In April, 1905, with the Lewis and Clark Exposition to open soon in Portland, a novel approach in advertising appeared in a large display:

"Ho! for the Exposition! is being advertised all over the East, but in this neck of the woods it is Ho! for H. O. Oliver's general merchandise store. Good quality and low prices are two of the characteristics of this business house."

In December, 1904, the Oliver family undertook an additional venture. An advertisement in the paper made the announcement:

Bakery

Fresh bread/Doughnuts/Pies and cakes

Mrs. Oliver/Houlton

at Harry O. Oliver's store

Mrs. Oliver's display ad appeared through January and into February, when it ceased to appear.

With no warning or explanation a large display advertisement in the May 19, 1905, *Columbia Register* announced the end of the Oliver store.

Closing out Sale

Our entire stock of $3,000 worth of fresh, clean goods going at cost. Come early while you have a good variety to select from. Remember this is the store where the dollars will count while the goods last.

H. O. Oliver

The advertisement was repeated in the May 26th paper and then disappeared.

The July 21, 1905, *Columbia Register* reprinted an evaluation of Houlton from the Portland *Telegram*: "Houlton is one of the liveliest little villages on the Pacific Coast, and does more business than towns triple its size. It is the distributing point for mail for nine villages, and its people are wide awake and up-to-date. There are three general merchandise stores—Perry and Graham, Brinn and Bailey, and Girty and Robey. The latter has recently purchased the large general merchandise store of Oliver. Both members of the firm are well and favorably known. . .the village is surrounded by splendid agricultural and fruit-bearing country. . .The great boon to Houlton is the mammoth plant of Western Cooperage Co. which employs 175 men.''

Thus in the pages of a village newspaper can be seen the rise and fall of an ambitious underfunded business enterprise while the town around it prospered. Houlton was doing well; the *Columbia Register* was not. After two years of publication, it, too, departed and Houlton and the surrounding area were again dependent on the *Oregon Mist* for local news. Girty and Robey, who bought out the Oliver stock, lasted in business only a couple of years.

Johnson's Landing on Scappoose bay was an early settlement at the south edge of the county. When the Northern Pacific Railway Company started building track toward Goble from Portland to connect with the Kalama-Tacoma track, William West donated land for a switching yard and a depot and at once plotted the town of Scappoose. The post office was moved to the railroad line and West opened a general store.

Harry West bought a quarter section of land northeast of the town, married Miss Eva Price in 1884, and began what was to develop into a prize-winning herd of Jersey cattle. West, over several years, made trips to the island of Jersey to bring back good stock. Even before the Lewis and Clark Exposition gave his herd an enviable name, his fine cattle were in demand.

Phillip Austin Frakes settled at Scappoose in 1883 and began raising registered Holstein cattle about 1887 on his Lakeside Farm. At the exposition he exhibited fourteen head of cattle, winning thirteen ribbons. In 1915 Frakes dedicated a modern dairy barn with an elaborate celebration. He chartered the steamer *America* to bring guests from St. Helens. A thousand people came from over the county with visitors from Washington and western Oregon. This occasion marked the thirty-eighth anniversary of the Frakes marriage. The Rev. Wm. Youngson, Methodist district superintendent from Portland, spoke. The Frakes, their new barn, and their fine herd of cattle were properly noticed in the press.

In 1900 the Honeyman farm began importing Ayreshire stock. Thus, Scappoose became the center for three varieties of registered dairy cattle.

Asa and Mary Holaday settled on fifteen acres of undeveloped land and built up the Monte Vista nursery, to supply the fruit trees and nursery stock needed by the farmers of the county. Asa Holaday, born in 1828, had crossed the plains by oxcart in 1853, and settled in Scappoose in 1883. His son A. D. Holaday, born in 1867, was in the family business. In November, 1898, the Holaday Nursery Company shipped eight tons of dried prunes and two carloads of apples to Colorado and other lots to Tacoma and Portland. In December, 1901, Holaday and Son shipped three carloads of apples to Denver.

The Holadays had a herd of dairy cattle as well as the nursery. Dairying in the area took precedent over fruit and diversified farming, but the orchards of the Holadays, Fred Dangerfield and others, were promising a good future for fruit growing.

In 1870, Scappoose was the most populated precinct in Columbia county, having 237 persons. In 1880, it had dropped in numbers to 168, but in 1900 it had 547 and in 1910, 649. Scappoose had two general merchandise stores, a blacksmith shop, I. G. Wikstrom's sawmill, and what the town called "the best school house in the county." It had cost $16,000. Scappoose organized the first Congregational church in the county and, as the community grew, a Methodist Episcopal church was built there also.

Warren, first named Gillton, like Scappoose on the railroad, developed first as a timber-harvesting section. It was heavily timbered from Scappoose bay to the hills. One of the early settlers was Merit F. Hazen, who bought timberland in 1879. He cut cordwood, cleared land, and developed general farming. Hazen sold fruit, vegetables, meat, butter and eggs in St. Helens. He was county assessor in 1883-1884 and a justice of the peace for six years. He sold his farm in Warren in 1908 and moved to St. Helens. Warren in the 1880s and 1890s was cordwood-cutting country. The timber could be handled easier in cordwood than in logs for mills, as streams were not available for floating the logs.

The Warren section developed general farming. The Washington Muckle farm specialized in horses, but the once timbered plains between the bay and the hills developed into orchards and fields of corn, oats, wheat, grasses and root vegetables. Wash Muckle took to the *Oregon Mist* office evidence of what the land would grow, displaying two carrots, each weighing five pounds, and two weighing four pounds each. His carrots yielded fifty-two tons per acre, worth ten dollars a ton for cattle feed. Corn was mostly cut green for ensilage.

Rural mail delivery made its initial appearance in Columbia county at Warren, beginning in 1904. Merchant Young sold sixty mail boxes the first summer. The Warren voting precinct had 588 persons in 1910, doubling the population in the decade. The Warren Methodist church struggled to stay alive for a few more years.

James S. Bacon was the Warren merchant and postmaster for many years. He had crossed the plains in 1852 when nine years old. He married in 1865 and had nine children. Bacon settled early in Warren, joining the St. Helens Masonic lodge in 1882. He died in September, 1915.

By the end of the first decade of the twentieth century the lowlands along the Columbia River between St. Helens and Clatsop county had been logged over. The rich timber harvest had brought into existence such localities as Neer City, Goble, Reuben, Stehman, Mayger, settlements dependent upon timber. Charles Mayger, Sr., had come to Columbia county in 1849, when St. Helens had but four men. He had helped clear out a road to the Scappoose plains from St. Helens before he settled in the area named for him. Thirty years of logging had moved the timber line back two, three or more miles to the hills and left thousands of acres of potentially rich farm land. Fishing and rock quarries were furnishing labor and income for some workers; however, cultivated fields were following close after the timber harvest. Logged-over land was offered for sale for from six to ten dollars an acre — "the best soil in the world" for fruit, grain or farm crops. Goble had a cold storage company to freeze fish for rail shipment. It also had orchards in which the Yellow Bellflower apple was outstanding — as the Northern Spy was at Scappoose.

Fishermen along the river in the first decade of the century were receiving five cents a pound for salmon, six cents for salmon over twenty-five pounds. A fisherman's outfit cost about four hundred dollars. The result of this investment was a gamble. Out of St. Helens in 1905 about ten sailing boats and thirty gasoline launches were fishing. The catch for the season came to about $35,000.

By 1890, the Clatskanie precinct had 624 population, though the town (incorporated in 1891) had only 212. Marshland had 180 people. The decade showed a good growth for the farm lands along the river. In 1900, by precincts, Marshland had 334 people, Clatskanie 888 (Clatskanie Town, 311), Goble 398, Deer Island 205, Oak Point 534, Beaver Falls 348. During the next decade Clatskanie precinct doubled, as did Goble and Deer Island and Oak Point. Marshland lost population, down to 242.

The county population in 1910 was 10,580.

Clatskanie started building a little before 1890 and developed rapidly. The 1880 census shows Clatskanie precinct with 146 people. In 1892, the town had six sawmills and many neat cottages. It was considering putting in a high school program as early as 1897. During that summer Clatskanie residents set aside a day to cut wood for the school. Men came with saws, axes, and wagons; women with food, coffee, and encouragement. Everyone had a frolic and more than enough wood for a year was cut and stacked. In 1900 the school opened with 104 pupils; in 1903 it had 127. By comparison, in 1900 Rainier had 120 pupils, St. Helens 43, Warren 54, Houlton 46.

Clatskanie in 1909, by Booster Club standards, was a city of 1,200, billing itself as the "gateway of the Nehalem." The census of 1910 found only 747 people. The Simon Benson logging operations had centered back of Clatskanie, where the largest logging camp in the county employed three hundred men when it was fully operative. The huge, seagoing cigar-shaped, Benson-developed, log rafts towed to San Diego out of the Columbia river were assembled at the Clatskanie river.

Large scale agriculture was beginning in the county in the Clatskanie area, in the lowlands between the town and the Columbia river. A Mr. Magruder was manager for the Columbia Agricultural Company, which set out to dike twelve thousand acres of the lowland.

Nehalem street, the main business street of the town, was also a first in the county. It was widened, straightened, improved with crushed rock, and oiled to keep down dust. This was an early venture into civic street improvement and urban renewal.

Nora and George Conger published a weekly newspaper, the *Chief*, which had begun publication in 1891. Clatskanie had a high school, electricity, a water system, and a creamery. Mist, up the Nehalem, also had a creamery.

One observer remarked about the Nehalem valley: "On all sides are to be seen unmistakable tokens of prosperity, happiness and contentment, where so recently it was but a wilderness." In fact, an average of ten or twelve teams a day used the road between Vernonia and Clatskanie.

Dr. James Withycombe of Oregon Agricultural College visited the Nehalem valley in the fall of 1907 and was pleased to note the development of fifty miles of farms along the valley streams. These inner county farms had developed in the face of frustration and disappointment by hardy and tenacious settlers. They had clamored for passable roads to market since, in 1879, they had hacked a road through the forest and over Bunker Hill toward St. Helens. Such a reasonably usable road did not connect Vernonia with the county seat for forty years. Talk of a railroad to market their timber products and to serve the valley began in the 1880s and continued to arouse expectations for a generation before it became a reality.

The Israel Spencer letters of 1876 and the Elmer Everett Nickerson diary of the early 1890s picture the early beginning of settled life around Vernonia.

The Nickersons were married in Kansas on October 26, 1887, when Everett was twenty-one, and on their third anniversary they were just moving into a new house in Vernonia. "Everett hung the kitchen door" on October 24th. In January Everett was finishing the bedroom and his wife was sewing on a first dress for a prospective baby. Everett went to the Literary Society meeting while his wife papered the closet. On Sunday she shaved Everett and gave him a bath; then she wrote letters. Mail came and went once a week from Houlton. On May thirteenth the Nickersons' ten pound baby boy was born, and a month later they had strawberry shortcake.

The Nickersons kept a hotel in Vernonia in 1890 and on for a time. Mrs. Nickerson went hop picking when the "fever" hit the valley. Nickerson started a sawmill in Vernonia in 1896. He took a load of hogs to Clatskanie to market in 1903, and he and his wife both took jobs in a Clatskanie mill that fall, she to cook for the crew.

Israel Spencer started his Vernonia farm in 1876. He had a "house 10 x 12, two acres cleared, ten acres chopped." He had planted beans, cabbage and tobacco. Spencer was better off than most of the new settlers; he had paid his way thus far and had thirteen twenty-dollar gold pieces left, but had yet to buy a cow. He was married a few years later and needed a bigger house. His son Omar was born in 1881.

Spencer was elected a county commissioner in 1888, serving four years. He was an activist in road agitation and prominent in church work, going to the county Sunday school convention and to the state meeting as a delegate. He developed a good farm with fine cattle.

Omar Spencer, along with Sid Malmsen, Doc Beeghley and Charles Mellinger, drove a herd of cattle from Vernonia to St. Helens, loading them on the steamer *Kellogg* for market in Cathlamet. This was in August, 1899. The next

View of Vernonia from east side of Rock creek, 1892

month Omar and Opal, children of Israel and Mrs. Spencer, went to Portland to attend the Methodist University of Portland. Omar sang in a quartet from the university, which performed admirably in St. Helens. "Columbia county people are proud of such a son," born and reared in Vernonia.

Omar entered Stanford University where he studied four years, coming home summers to work on farms. In the summer of 1902, the Spencer children, Omar, Opal, Maggie and Rob, took a load of wool and other produce to Forest Grove to market, their first such trip on their own without their father. At the 1904 Fourth of July celebration, a proud Vernonia had its native son, Omar Spencer, then a Stanford University senior, deliver the oration of the day. When Columbia county observed its centennial celebration in 1954, this same Omar Spencer, prominent Portland lawyer, was the orator of the day.

Israel Spencer and his family were well-liked in the community. At New Year's, for 1897 and 1898, the Spencers hosted dinners for many of their friends at their cattle farm.

Vernonia had its merchants, its craftsmen, its school and church, plus the most actively continuous literary society in the county. The annual August camp meeting of the Evangelical Association was an outstanding county event.

In 1870 there were no Nehalem valley residents, but the 1880 census shows an Auburn and Nehalem precinct with 362 people. In 1890 Auburn precinct had 528, Nehalem 472. In 1900 an Apiary precinct was formed with 87 people; Auburn, including Vernonia, had 490. The town of Vernonia had 62 residents. In 1910 Apiary had 108, Auburn precinct 413, Vernonia town 69 (included in Auburn precinct).

In the early days of ox teams and pack horses, logging and timber harvest could not develop very far from a food supply for men and beasts, and water transportation for wood products. Along the streams of the inner county, farms emerged as the timber fell. Half a dozen houses became a settlement. Pittsburg, Mist, Natal, Apiary developed. What delayed the settlement of this interior valley was the lack of roads — its inaccessibility. Under the circumstances the VanBlaricoms, Mellingers, Randles, Parkers, Weeds and all showed great adaptability and fortitude in making a town, in developing the valley area.

After the Muckle mill burned in 1904, St. Helens was without a sawmill for five years. During those five years the town grew very little from its 258 population in 1900. The Muckle mill site and a mile of waterfront was bought by the Charles R. McCormick Company in October, 1908. The company built a thousand feet of lumber dock and operated five steamships of its own in addition to loading vessels for other companies. In April, 1910, the company shipped out a million board feet of lumber per day for ten consecutive days — ten million feet of lumber in ten days. The ships, *Alvina, King Cyrus, Bangor, Virginia, Jewell, Marhoffer, Casco, Stetsos, Saginaw, Yellowstone, Shoshone, Yosemite, Klamath*, all loaded lumber at the McCormick dock during the ten days. The usual run was about five million a month.

The McCormick Company bought out the C. C. Masten interests on Milton creek in September — four thousand acres of timber land, ten miles of logging railroad, nine donkey engines, two Shay locomotives, thirty-six logging trucks — for about a half million dollars. C. C. Masten was continued as operator and manager of the logging operation, the St. Helens Logging Company.

When, in November, the new city hall for St. Helens was dedicated — "the finest public building between Portland and the mouth of the Columbia River" — H. F. McCormick invited 250 people to a celebrating supper, ball, and card party.

St. Helens was undergoing a period of growth and development even more pronounced than Rainier's earlier expansion. With the New Year's issue to begin 1913, the editor of the *Oregon Mist* could rejoice in the good year just past — new industries, additional businesses, new residences, miles of improved streets, new sewers, ship-building, the creosote plant, a new sawmill [the Columbia

County Lumber Company built a small mill] — "Prosperity and development shows on every hand." St. Helens and Houlton were to consolidate into one city government in January, 1913.

In September, 1912, the St. Helens school opened the year with seven teachers and 250 pupils. Before the school year had gone very far a new teacher was added. In 1909 three teachers taught eighty pupils. In 1910 four teachers had 120 pupils. In 1911 five teachers started the year but a sixth was added during the year.

A new St. Helens schoolhouse, the John Gumm school, was dedicated January 18, 1912. John Gumm came to the river community in 1854, a single man with no known relatives. When he died in Columbia City in 1883, his small estate was left to two districts for building schools. Today's John Gumm school building was built in 1919, the one dedicated in 1912 having burned in the fall of 1918.

St. Helens had twenty-four pupils enrolled in the high school in 1912, two of them seniors. Yankton school had started the first two years of high school a couple of years earlier.

The increase in school population reflected the growth of the city. The population of St. Helens in 1908 was about 400; in 1910 about 750; in 1912 about 1,500, according to an October estimate, and about 2,500, according to an exaggerated December estimate. The county was thought to have a population of 15,000.

XI: FARMING

From the fact that upon agriculture rests the prosperity of a country, and the sustenance of life itself, it is apparent that agriculture is the most important of all occupations.

May, 1906, Committee on Agriculture,
Oregon State Grange Proceedings

The American ideal from the beginning of the nation was to own and till land. As settlers moved westward, farming land was not only an ideal, it was also a necessity. The two letters written by Israel Spencer from Vernonia in 1876 document the agricultural beginning in the Nehalem valley. After a summer of chopping, in August he had two acres of land cleared and twelve acres chopped. Clearing out the big trees was a formidable undertaking. "We have to burn down the trees here. Some of them are six and eight feet through; to burn them in two, bore with an augur, start the fire, and let them rip." He had cabbage, beans and tobacco planted that summer.

By November, with more land ready, he was planting winter oats. "First you take a grub hoe and go down in the woods and see how long it will take you to grub up enough ground to seed two bushels of oats and one of wheat. Then take a rake and rake it in. That is the way I am doing it this winter . . ."

Spencer was enthusiastic over the prospect for farming. He did not, surrounded by three-hundred-foot-high trees, mention lumbering. "The crops are the best here that I ever saw. In this valley the soil . . . is the richest dirt that I ever saw. Wheat, oats and garden stuff grow beyond all account.'' Israel Spencer, over the following years, developed a fine farm and reared a family in that inner county valley.

The five families living in Vernonia in 1875 organized a school district — No. 12 in the county — and in 1876 built a school of hewn logs. Ogais Cherrington was the first teacher —for whose daughter, Vernonia, the town was named. Thirty-nine people cast votes in the June election of 1879. In 1879, some Nehalem valley men slashed the wagon road, really a mere wagon trail, over Bunker Hill to connect with the road into St. Helens.

Settling the inner county came slowly. In February, 1887, Robert Frye and wife moved to their Carico valley homestead. An editorial in the *Oregon Mist*, October 30, 1891, urged that more settlers were needed. ''We have more good land subject to homestead entry than any other county in the state.''

Early in the 1890s farms were starting up Milton creek, into Carico valley, Spring valley, on to Pittsburg, Mist, Apiary. The soil was good, the climate was good, hopeful settlers were coming. Nearer the river, at Deer Island, an observer wrote in January, 1892: ''Though times are very dull and cash scant, yet the industrious farmers seem prosperous: fields are being cleared and orchards planted, new barns and houses are being built.'' Many, if not most of the settlers, built their own houses and barns.

The Yankton correspondent commented on neighborhood building in progress and summed up: ''Yankton is keeping step with the other progressive neighborhoods of our county along the line of improvements, chiefly noticeable by fresh paint, new fences, enlarged fields and a general air of thrift and content among the burghers.''

Columbia county in 1894 had 12,000 acres of land under cultivation; 63,284 bushels of potatoes were reported and 8,235 bushels of apples and pears. Farming was beginning, but it was far out-distanced by timber products.

All through the 1890s reports from rural correspondents gave accounts of acres being slashed, slashings being burned, fields being cleared, barns being built, fences being put up and stumps being taken out one by one. Columbia county land had a lot of stumps.

By the end of the decade, Herb Howard was using blasting powder and a remodeled tractor engine and chain to get some of his fields cleared. Fifteen years after the Yankton schoolhouse was built the stumps were finally cleared from the school grounds. Not until 1910 were the stumps cleared from the road right-of-way between Houlton and Yankton. Clearing out stumps was a slow process.

Toward the end of the 1890s pigs came into the Milton creek news, pigs for market. Howard shipped twenty hogs to the Portland market for a good price. G. R. Hyde marketed a "prime lot of pork" which he had successfully raised out-of-doors. Fred E. Oliver offered young pigs for sale.

The 1880 census for Columbia county reported that only sixty gallons of milk were sent to a creamery during the year, but that 46,908 pounds of butter were made on the farms. The census showed 877 milk cows, and 1,053 other cattle. Some farmers made butter to sell to mill and camp boarding houses and also supplied meat to the cooks. The Tarbells at Yankton in 1901 opened a small creamery, buying milk from the farmers around and selling butter to the camps up Milton creek.

Cattle received attention in the county. The West Jersey farm in Scappoose developed. Fred Briggs at Yankton bought two Jersey heifers and Israel Spencer in Vernonia bought one of West's Jerseys for his own developing dairy herd. Herb Howard bought a thoroughbred red poll bull for his herd of beef cattle.

Harry West, for 1899, kept details on eight milking Jerseys. They averaged 6,775 pounds of milk each cow, with 428 pounds of butter. Each cow earned $79.68 for the year. He sold a three-months-old calf to A. C. Ray of Rainier for $45.

D. W. Freeman of Rock creek, in February, 1900, sold three head of steers for $170. Good cows were scarce and sold for $35 to $45. Horses sold for $100 to $125.

H. H. Clark at Warren introduced a new element into the county farming picture. He employed ten Japanese on his farm, teaching some of them to milk cows. Others did general farm work and land clearing. Unfortunately, after some months there, one of them drowned in Scappoose bay. Clark praised them as dependable, steady workers, eager to learn and "not dissatisfied with their wages."

Chickens and eggs, too, came into the Milton creek picture in the late 1890s, with the Perrys and Charles Tarbell both promoting settings of eggs and chickens for sale. The Rev. R. B. Mason of Yankton developed a rabbitry, featuring Belgian hares.

The United States census reports give a generalized picture of the development of Columbia county agriculture and the diversified products turned out by a basically homogenous population. In 1890 the county had 358 farms averaging 222 acres, 339 of the farms cultivated by their owners. Twelve farms were rented for a fixed sum and seven were rented on shares. The meaning of the words *improved* and *unimproved* land must have changed over the decades, for the 1890 census reports more improved farm land in the county than does the 1900 census, even though over the decade active land clearing was continuously being reported. The 358 farms in 1890 reported 20,000 improved acres and 60,000 unimproved acres. In 1900 eight hundred farms averaging 178 acres each had only 18,045 acres of improved land. Of these, 663 farms were cultivated by owners, 53 had cash-paying tenants and 26 sharecroppers.

The 1910 census showed 813 farms in the county, an increase of only twelve for the decade. Of these, 713 were farmed by the owners, 87 by tenants and 13 by resident managers. In 1910, of the 813 farms, 546 were reported free from debt, 167 mortgaged. By 1910 the improved farm area had decreased again to 16,000 acres, about twenty acres per farm. The average size of farms in the county decreased decade by decade, from the 222 acres in 1890 to 90 acres in 1920 and 71 acres in 1930. The 813 farms in the county in 1910 were farmed by 469 native born whites, 343 foreign born whites, and one non-white.

When Francis Perry had sawed the timber on his claim on Perry creek in the 1850s, he planted fruit trees as other settlers did. The 1890 census reported 8,824 bearing apple trees, 657 cherry trees, 108 peach trees, 623 pear trees, and 1,974 prune or plum trees. The county also had a variety of bush and vine small fruits. By 1900 the county had 42,666 bearing apple trees, 7,741 cherry trees, 555 peach trees, 6,670 pear trees. The 1910 census cut down the number of fruit trees considerably: 21,048 bearing apple trees, merely one-half the number reported a decade earlier. In like manner cherry and pear trees were reduced about one-half to 3,546 cherry and 3,488 pear. Prune and plum trees were 7,777. Twenty thousand quarts of strawberries were reported harvested in the county in 1909.

Over the twenty years from 1890 to 1910, the dairy produce of the county doubled. In 1890 two thousand milk cows produced 600,000 gallons of milk, with 158,077 pounds of butter made on the farms. The 1900 census listed 685 farms reporting dairy products, one and one-half million gallons of milk produced, of which 166,880 gallons were sold. Butter amounting to 196,532 pounds was made on farms, 101,033 pounds sold. Some cheese was reported made and sold.

The 1910 census reported 4,515 dairy cattle, one and a half million gallons of milk produced, one-third million gallons sold; 94,249 pounds of butter produced, 26,733 pounds sold. About this time three or four creameries were starting in the county.

The number of sheep reported was never large, the maximum being 2,500 in 1900. The 1890 census reported that seventy-seven sheep were killed by dogs in 1889. Chickens increased from 10,000 in 1890 to 25,000 in 1910. A hundred and fifty thousand dozen eggs were laid, eighty thousand dozen sold.

Bees produced 20,000 pounds of honey in 1900.

Fruit and Columbia county went together from the beginning. Small berries, vine berries, fruit trees were thought of as doing well in the soil and climate. People from New England were astonished at the lushness and size and flavor of the various fruits. Prunes did so well at Yankton that both Fred Briggs and Charles Tarbell put in their own dryers to care for their crops in 1895. The Holady Nursery Company of Scappoose dried and sold prunes by the ton and shipped carloads of apples to market from Scappoose before the decade ended. Prunes sold for four or four and a half cents a pound. Potatoes in the spring of 1899 sold for $1.50 a sack.

The Patrons of Husbandry, or the local grange chapters, began to serve a serious purpose in the county with the beginning of the new century. Grangers were interested in substantial permanent community development, roads, buildings, farms, and women's work in the home.

The grange movement began in Oregon in 1873 with the first chapter organized at Marshfield in Clackamas county, and chapters following rapidly in the Willamette valley. A state grange was organized in Salem, September 24, 1873, with thirty-seven local chapters having been already organized that summer. The first resolution passed by the state grange was a plea for improved water navigation. Valley farmers wanted to get their produce to market. No mention was made of roads. In 1874 190 new grange chapters were added, and by 1875 the grange in Oregon and Washington territory claimed 10,885 members. That sudden growth exploded in conflict of interest and political infighting; by 1881 the grange in the Northwest had only 1,440 members and many of the chapters had disappeared.

The grange came to Columbia county with the twentieth century. The Vail grange at Warren, No. 294 in the state, was the first significant chapter in the county, reporting to the annual state meeting in May, 1901, that its officers were Mrs. Ruth A. Hout, Miss Maud Stevens and Miss Lillian Larsen — a slate of women officers. Its organization was soon followed by several in the county: No. 301 at Yankton,

302 at Natal, 303 at Scappoose, 305 at Vernonia, 306 at Beaver Valley, 320 at Cedar Grove, 321 at Clatskanie, 326 at Rainier, 327 at Quincy, 329 at Goble, 332 at Mayger, 334 at Deer Island, 337 at Fishhawk. Five more chapters were organized much later, and some of the earlier chapters did not thrive.

The organizing members of the Vernonia chapter were the Wilsons, Shanahans, Schoonovers, Sheldelins, Dows, Mellingers, Wilkinsons, Malmstens, Pringles, Mills, Nergersons, Tucker, Sheeley, and E. Geesel, who was the first master, and his wife, who was the secretary.

At the state meeting in 1903 Columbia county was represented by fourteen local grange chapters, in 1905 by twelve chapters, and in 1930 by twelve chapters — but not the same twelve. The grange fluctuated in stability from community to community and from year to year. However, over the first quarter of the twentieth century grange chapters were of great importance in the development and permanent settlement of the inner county. The Yankton, Natal, Vernonia, and Beaver Valley grange chapters were probably consistently the most stable, most active, most progressive forces in the back county.

The 1903 state grange meeting asked for free rural mail delivery, pure food laws, and the direct election of senators.

Yankton grange No. 301 was organized in August, 1901, by a Mr. Castro of Clackamas county. The charter members were Lawrence and Emma Tarbell, Fred Briggs, Rudolph Kappler, Frank Brown, Mr. and Mrs. G. R. Hyde, and Gordon C. Barger, who was elected the first master. Fred Briggs was the secretary.

The grange in December, 1902, elected officers for the next year. Rudolph Kappler was the new master. The grange was ready to exert an influence, and sponsored the building of a community hall that summer. The telephone line was stretched from Ross's drug store in St. Helens to the Yankton post office and grocery store, and the Baptist church was built in Yankton that same summer.

In October, 1903, the Yankton grange held an all day meeting on the subject "How to Make a Farm Pay." The meeting was planned also as a demonstration, with a display of fruits, potatoes, squash, pumpkins, rutabegas, turnips, cabbage, carrots, and corn stalks.

Lawrence Tarbell was appointed to start the discussion. The session was lively, with contributions and talks by many people. George W. Perry and his wife both spoke. Mrs. Perry spoke of raising beans and children. She advocated livestock and poultry. Others making suggestions were Rudolph Kappler, Gordon C. Barger, Christ Jensen, Charles Tarbell, Frank Brown, Iris Oliver, George Crosby, May Briggs, Fred Franz, Mrs. G. R. Hyde.

The meeting had a supper and a program. Song and recitation were standard parts of the rural program. Singing were C. C. Moyer, Fred and Clara Franz and Leland Hyde. Recitations were by Rudolph Kappler, Mrs. Kate Perry, George Hyde, Iris Oliver, Nettie Charlton; readings by Lawrence Tarbell, Mrs. G. R. Hyde. Christ Jensen played his violin.

This occasion marked the earliest display of farm products in the county. It preceded the first "fair" by five years. In 1904 the Oregon legislature voted to fund the Lewis and Clark Exposition in Portland and the idea of an agricultural fair began to be talked of in the county. The 1905 Lewis and Clark Exposition gave agriculture a boost in Columbia county, as it added impetus to general Oregon development. All summer the county's depots were selling train tickets to Portland.

Columbia county had the problem of protecting its valuable crops from destructive insects. The question of individual freedom while enforcing standardizing was a crucial one for the farmer in this century's first decade. There was need for a standard size for the marketed box of apples, and a need for apple grades. One wormy apple cast a shadow over others, and one infested orchard could endanger a community. The editor of the *Oregon Mist* wrote under the heading "Wormy Apples," August 25, 1905, "the only way to stop people from marketing bad apples is by a strict system of inspection and condemnation. All over the state wormy apples are offered for sale, that should have been fed to the hogs . . . The spread of the coddling moth must be curtailed to save the orchards. Enforce the laws." But, he insisted, Columbia county apples were as good as any in the state and even better in that the county had less fruit disease.

All up and down the inner county were signs that settlers, even though the men folk worked in logging or mills, were looking toward developing farms and expanding agricultural production. The valley showed great versatility. Charles Tarbell was proud of his poultry development. Hyde was marketing poultry; Howard and others, hogs. Gordon Barger advertised a Morgan stallion kept on stud at $5 a guaranteed service, and Herb Howard also advertised a stud.

Mr. Stevens named his farm "Milton Park" as it overlooked the big bend in the creek below Howard's farm. He emphasized strawberries on his hillside acreage, harvesting "a fairly good crop." The picking engaged six or eight people for twelve days. Charles Tarbell wrote in 1910 that one of his neighbors had four acres of strawberries, "which will probably net in the neighborhood of $1,000." Lawrence and Ray Tarbell each set out a half acre of strawberries.

"The apple harvest here is exceptionally fine. No other section of the state produces a better quality of apples than this part [Yankton] of Columbia county." Lawrence Tarbell harvested 300 boxes of apples in 1910, sending half of them to the St. Louis market.

In August, 1906, Yankton could report that "all kinds of grain have done well and harvesting is nearly completed. Fruit is in prime condition and all kinds except prunes are abundant."

Frank Brown fit up a threshing machine in 1906 and, for ten years or more, the Brown thresher, whether operated by Frank or Perley or Eber, became a part of the surrounding scene. A decade earlier Fred Zeller was running a threshing machine for the farmers in the Valley area.

Perley Brown running his early Yankton threshing machine about 1909. Charlie Bushong is facing the engine.

Interest in the Agricultural Pavilion and the cattle displays at the Lewis and Clark Exposition was pronounced. Columbia county publicized not only its timber products, but also its cattle herds, fruit and diversified farming. There was talk of organizing a county fair, but nothing came of it until the Yankton grange held its own fair in September, 1908. The county was invited to participate and attend. Most of the exhibitors, however, were Milton creek residents.

In October, 1909, the Yankton grange held its second fall fair, regarded by all observers as an outstanding success for the county. Luigi Rosasco took first on vegetables. Rosasco was an Italian immigrant truck farmer with a family who was making a place for himself in the community. Several years later he organized the Italian Importing Company and built a three story building between Houlton and St. Helens, a landmark for sixty years.

Editor Flagg of the *Oregon Mist*, a promoter of the fair idea, wrote, "Especially notable was the entire exhibit from Ray Tarbell's ten acre farm, including as it did 35 varieties of canned fruits and vegetables.'' Tarbell came to Yankton at age eight in 1892 with his family from Arookstook county, Maine. He attended Yankton school, married Florence Nowles when he was twenty, and bought the ten acre farm from his grandfather, Charles Tarbell. He was the first and possibly only farmer of his generation along Milton creek to live entirely from his farm. He neither worked out nor made outside investments. Tarbell used diversified farming with intensive cultivation. He raised as much of his chicken feed as he could, sold eggs and breeding stock. For his dairy cows he raised sugar beets and ensilage. He had, as Editor Flagg noted, a variety of fruits and vegetables. He used the name, Intervale Poultry Farm, and developed flocks in various breeds.

Frank Brown wrote for the *Pacific Homestead* an article on how he made a thousand dollars on his farm in a year. He had in March, 1908, six dairy cows, ten intended for beef, twenty-eight shoats, forty Barred Rock hens. He grew to feed his livestock an acre of kale, an acre and a half of carrots, a half acre of sugar beets, turnips, sweet corn. He also had a team of horses. Although this farm yielded him a thousand dollars, he thought it could do even better.

Lawrence Tarbell took the lead in organizing the Yankton Fruit Growers Association, and in 1910 the association shipped 900 boxes of apples to St. Paul, Minnesota. Someone wrote, ''There is no business a young man can go into that is more certain to insure him a competence than apple-growing in the Yankton and Bachelor Flat neighborhood.''

The Yankton grange's fifth agricultural fair in September, 1912, brought participants from a more wide-ranging area. The fair had exhibits for women and children as well as for general farm showings. The list of ribbon and prize money winners was extensive.

The next year the grange-sponsored fair was merged into a county fair, under the presidency of Lawrence Tarbell. A fairgrounds was developed at St. Helens, and the 1913 event was a genuine county fair. Ray Tarbell of Yankton was the outstanding exhibitor. He placed in various produce entries

Cassilda Wilwerding and Ralph Tarbell at the Yankton school. Note top buggy in background. The Jersey cow would indicate that this occasion is at the Yankton grange fair, probably 1911.

The first agricultural show in Columbia county was held by the Yankton Grange No. 303 in September, 1908. Photograph was taken outside Yankton grange hall, which had an outside stairway to the second floor. Small girl at extreme right is Marie Walker Poff, daughter of the Nathan Walkers. Tree snags remained on grounds.

and swept all the ribbons in Barred Plymouth Rock poultry, receiving about $90 in prize money. Lawrence Tarbell and Frank Brown followed closely with about $75 each.

Pittsburg was mostly unsettled farms, deserted residences and empty buildings by 1910. Peris had lost its post office in 1901 with Valley taking over the mail of that area. The Canaan post office also had been closed and soon the Valley office was closed. Into the vacuum came the community of Trenholm. It developed on Milton creek near the headquarters of the Western Cooperage Company's forest operation. The Western Cooperage bolt camp and various wood cutters had operated in the district irregularly since 1904. However, the development of Trenholm was different. The Western Cooperage boom was over and families were settling in with the thought of permanence. Trenholm had a sawmill, too.

The local scribe, a man of wit, spoke of the new settlement: "Trenholm is several hundred acres of fertile land ten miles west of St. Helens and is bounded on the east by sunshine, on the south by warm winds, on the north by strawberries, and on the west by honey and cream, which makes it a very desirable place to live." John Wilwerding's farm with its many hives of bees was to the west.

Among the early homesteaders were the Fowlers and George Wilson, who came with his family in 1908 to work as a teamster in the area. Mrs. Wilson, finding no school at Trenholm, took a temporary teaching certificate and opened a school with eight pupils in the fall of 1909.

In another news note the local correspondent said, "We have had several chances lately to have factories of different kinds locate here at Trenholm, but they make so much confusion with their whistles, we concluded we didn't want them, but referred them to the St. Helens Commercial Club and told them their headquarters was in that new wooden structure with the mudholes in front. In case they should move their headquarters or the mud hole we would like to be notified." St. Helens was undergoing considerable industrial expansion in 1912.

Mrs. George Wilson, teacher at the first Trenholm school in 1909, and her pupils. Her son Max is beside her; Harry at far left. Three Fowler daughters of an early homesteading family are in group.

The anonymous Trenholm booster also wrote: "Mr. Walter Duff returned from Tillamook a few days ago and is talking some of moving to Tillamook. I don't see how anyone can think of leaving a place like Trenholm and move to a little place like Tillamook." Walter Duff did leave Trenholm, at least for a time, to build a house on some lots he owned in Portland. Henry Peters, "our popular chicken fancier, has sold over a thousand eggs" over six weeks. O.D. Kyle moved to St. Helens. "The reason he gave for moving was that there was too much excitement here."

The reporter wrote that Fred Floeter, who lived up on Bunker Hill, said he shot a cougar that was twenty-seven feet long and an inch high and had three rows of teeth and holes punched for more. "As we have never caught Fred monkeying with the truth we believe it."

The week later: "We would like to change our item of last week in regard to Fred Floeter's cougar; in fact, Fred was down and interviewed us. After we had dragged ourself from the piles of rubbish behind the post office and removed the decayed wood from our eyes we agreed with Fred that the cougar we mentioned was out of proportion."

At the end of June, 1911, the Trenholm Sunday school put on an entertainment. F. J. McAboy was the superintendent, assisted by Mrs. Anna Randle, Mrs. Mode Griffith, Mrs. Effie Wilson, Mrs. Frank Tatroe and W. J. Hinston. Children taking part were Ruth Fowler, Max Wilson, Clifford Fowler, Harry Wilson, Matilda Johnston, Wilbur Larabee, Albert and Ella Kelley, Ada Johnston. Mrs. N. O. Larabee, wife of the Trenholm postmaster, had a part in the festivities.

The community held a Thanksgiving dinner in the old bolt camp mess hall of the Western Cooperage Company. After the dinner they went to the schoolhouse for Thanksgiving exercises, giving the school pupils of Mrs. Effie Wilson a chance to demonstrate. Mrs. Wilson was giving splendid satisfaction as a teacher. Her sons, Harry and Max, were about twelve and nine years old. George Wilson and his wife and family had come from Michigan. Effie gave private lessons on the piano as well as teaching the school. Marie

The Trenholm sawmill about 1911. This mill was distinct from the Western Cooperage Company's stave mill, which began shipping out staves in 1913.

Walker took her younger sister Lena from Yankton to Trenholm for Saturday music lessons.

George Wilson was driving the Trenholm-Houlton stage in 1912 and working in the bolt camp in 1913. He was proud of his flock of Plymouth Rock hens, which he had bought from Than Brown at Yankton. Wilson was once again carrying the mail on the Milton creek route. Effie taught the Trenholm school for two years before accepting "a more lucrative offer" to be the Yankton principal. George Wilson was a familiar figure up and down the south county buying cattle to sell to the Portland market.

The Larabees had been neighbors of the Wilsons in Michigan and came to the community in 1910. N. O. Larabee opened a general store and established the post office, named after a town in Michigan. Larabee was the postmaster.

A new schoolhouse was constructed, which, remodeled, was in use as a family residence in 1982. The Western Cooperage Company was selling off its logged-over land in ten acre lots. New settlers were coming into the valley. Trenholm had roads in fair condition between it and St. Helens. From Trenholm to Vernonia the ten miles were still undeveloped.

In October, 1913, Trenholm organized a telephone company. There were sixty people belonging to the library and literary association. Meetings were lively and hopes were high. The Trenholm Orchard Company seemed to promise a future. The Rev. C. L. Dark, the Methodist minister in Houlton, held regular services in Trenholm. It seemed certain to many people that the eventual automobile road from Portland to the coast would go up Milton creek through Trenholm and Pittsburg.

Trenholm mushroomed for a few years, putting up cabins for wood cutters and mill workers; but the scene changed. The mill burned, the bolt camp vanished, the Western Cooperage Company moved to St. Johns. N. O. Larabee, the postmaster, moved to Houlton where he kept the hotel, the Houlton House, and the adjoining livery stable. The George Wilsons moved to St. Helens, where Effie Wilson taught in

The Trenholm bolt camp, about 1910.

the John Gumm school. The McAboy brothers closed their shingle mill.

The once thriving Polish settlement around the St. Joseph Catholic church vanished and the land returned to forest. Trenholm, too, almost vanished as the growing timber largely took over. The entire St. Helens-Vernonia axis which had once seemed headed for farm land was again largely returning to timber.

XII: AUTOMOBILES COME TO THE COUNTY

*Two events occurred in 1908 that were to be of lasting
significance . . . William C. Durant . . . formed the
General Motors Company . . . and Henry Ford announced
the Model T.*

Alfred P. Sloan, Jr.

When considered over a sufficient period of time, life can
be seen to change, even to develop in a distinguishable
direction. In the short range of a day or a month, the life of
Columbia county might be said to move barely. Charles
Tarbell wrote in October, 1911, "There is so few changes
among us there don't seem to be much to write about." But
at the same time his daughter, Alice Brown, wrote, "This
part of the country is changing rapidly."

Within walking range of Alice Brown and her aging
father, the locomotive whistle sounded as the train chugged
its load of logs to the mill where a mere decade before oxen
had skidded logs to Milton Creek for sluicing downstream.
An occasional automobile struggled by on a graded and
partly graveled road where earlier horse and driver had
striven to avoid mud ruts.

Little by little, almost imperceptibly, change had
modified the county. Roads, schools, churches, homes,
barns, orchards, cleared fields, herds of cattle, and social
organizations had appeared. By 1915, the county fair was
visited by a congressman, the governor, and a flying
machine. One could go from St. Helens to Portland on an
automobile stage. An ambitious youngster could be
prepared to enter college in a rudimentary high school at
four different centers in the county.

However, Columbia county had its problems. An editorial in the August 28, 1914, issue of the *St. Helens Mist* outlined and deplored the situtation: "No county in the State of Oregon was ever so badly torn up by sectional and factional strife as is Columbia county at the present time. It has all come about as a result of the determination of the people to build a system of roads in the county. Each locality has its own conception and idea of just how that road should be built, where it should run and how much money should be put on its particular section of road . . ."

Roads. Roads. Roads. What is more important to the social system than the means of intercommunication? Pioneers still living in 1915 had helped clear a trail from the Scappoose plains to the county seat at St. Helens. Judson Weed and others still living talked about volunteer workers cutting the wagon road over Bunker Hill from Vernonia to St. Helens. Clatskanie, Rainier and Deer Island all clamored for roads to open up their hinterlands and develop their communities.

And the automobile came. The automobile gradually edged up on the state and on Columbia county. Helmos W. Thompson of Eugene was recorded on May 19, 1905, as the first automobile owner in the state. Four of the first ten recorded automobiles were owned in Eugene, three in Salem, one in Woodburn, one in Arlington. The tenth car recorded was owned in Portland. N. A. Perry registered a Reo automobile, April 12, 1909, number 1529 in the state, the first in Columbia county. Dr. Harry R. Cliff of St. Helens followed on May 24, recording a Tourist, manufactured in Los Angeles, number 1788 in the state, second in the county.

The state first imposed a license fee on motor vehicles in 1907, when 236 vehicles, including motorcycles, were licensed for a total of $708 in fees. In 1918, licensing fees were increased and the state collected $802,229 in 1919, and over two million dollars in 1920. There were 103,790 automobiles licensed in that year.

A citizen of St. Helens wrote a letter to the *St. Helens Mist* in 1921 asking the question: "Are we auto mad?" He answered his own question with supporting argument. Yes, the county, the state, has gone auto mad. For the sake of purchasing automobiles people are neglecting farm needs, farm development, family needs, family education. People are mortgaging homes, going in debt, endangering their futures all for automobiles which they do not need. The city, the county — the people are automobile mad.

And they were mad in a different sense about roads.

In the summer of 1910 Portlanders were heating up talk of a highway from Portland to the ocean. Plans were drafted for a highway through Columbia county by way of St. Helens, Yankton, Pittsburg, Mist and on into Clatsop county. Pittsburg was even expected to be a manufacturing city of importance on this highway, with water power and timber. The interior county was excited over the Portland-initiated project, but the plans died on the preliminary drafting board.

Multnomah county had about forty per cent of the automobiles in the state in 1914. Multnomah and Marion counties together had almost half of the registered vehicles. In the summer of 1914 Columbia county had 70 automobiles, Clatsop county 219, Clackamas county 408, Washington county 357. Registration figures for the state showed 3,688 Fords, one Napier.

A dozen automobiles were owned in the county by the end of 1910. The owners and recorded numbers in the state were Henry Newman, Scappoose, a Reo (3161); James Muckle, St. Helens (3508); L. R. Rutherford, St. Helens, a Chalmers (3737); E. E. Nickerson, Vernonia, International Harvester (4148); George W. Kelley, St. Helens saloon keeper, a Ford (4246); Morton and Stort, St. Helens, a truck (4509); Christ Johnson and son, Clatskanie, White (4655); Willys Kelley, Deer Island, Hendee motorcycle (4683); Milton Smith, Rainier, a Buick (4707); D. W. Price, Scappoose, a Cadillac (5003).

Locally owned automobiles were mentioned in the *Oregon Mist* during 1910 with increasing frequency in 1911 and later. The Muckles drove by auto to Tillamook without trouble and had a splendid time. This was a week's trip. W. B. Dillard, the lawyer, had a new dark green Marion automobile. The L. R. Rutherfords and the William Rosses drove in Rutherford's car to the annual conference of the Methodist Episcopal church in Salem. Rutherford's auto was involved in a horse and buggy accident on a narrow grade.

The conflict between horse and buggy and the automobile was very real during a decade of transition. Alice and Frank Brown had a driving horse and a buggy of which they were very fond. As automobiles came into more common use Alice wrote that Nellie was "so afraid of autos in the night as to be hardly safe." She and Frank walked the two miles to grange rather than drive at night.

When the Rutherfords went to visit the Nehalem valley they went by way of the Germantown road and Buxton. The editor of the *St. Helens Mist* in 1913 rode with Mr. and Mrs. McCormick in their Buick into the Nehalem valley from St. Helens going by way of the Germantown road through Centerville, Roy, Banks, Crawford's Mill, Buxton, Kist, Vernonia, to Pittsburg, going seventy-seven miles to cover the twenty-one miles between Pittsburg and St. Helens. It was, the editor wrote, mostly pretty bad road, rutty, dusty, ungraded, with some hills twelve to fifteen per cent grades.

In 1912 John Johnson bought a seven-passenger White automobile for the Houlton-St. Helens jitney run. His car had electric lights, a self-starter, an electric siren that sounded like a steamer fog horn. In April, 1913, the Johnsons — father and sons — drove a new Winton Six down from Portland. The firm then had four automobiles. They had been in the transportation business six months: they did taxi service, met the trains, hauled baseball players to games and met other special needs. An auto ride from Portland to St. Helens in one hour and ten minutes made headline news that summer.

By September, 1913, an automobile bus was running a regular passenger schedule between Portland and St. Helens, one trip a day, one hour forty-five minutes each way. The St. Helens-Portland Auto Company established its Portland terminal at Meier and Frank's, with rest rooms, a check room and a public telephone. The bus made two round trips daily for the Rose Festival week.

George Konopica used an automobile to make deliveries on his milk route. In April, 1914, the county bought a truck to haul gravel, maintaining for justification that it could do the work of five teams and five men. The *St. Helens Mist* in May, 1914, published a Home and Farm magazine section, which included an "Automobile and Good Roads" feature. The Columbia City school closed its year with a picnic, furnishing ice cream and cake and giving the students automobile rides as a treat. A May 30 newspaper item announced that Don Smith had a hundred gallon tank of gasoline and was prepared to supply any passers-by.

Automobiles became more common, but car sales still made local news. Fords sold well in 1915, the St. Helens dealer selling seven in the first three months of the year. In August the Ford Motor Company sent checks of fifty dollars to all purchasers of Ford cars during the year. The county bought a Ford for use of the county road supervisor.

Automobiles needed roads. The question of priority in the expenditure of road funds became paramount: a subject for differences, for argument, for cantankerous name-calling. Puncheon roads, rutted mud roads, ungraded snake-like wagon trails still made up a considerable part of the five hundred miles of road in Columbia county.

Columbia county voted on February 6, 1914, on a bond issue of $360,000 to improve roads. In the weeks before the election the question of where to spend the money was hotly debated. The Portland press and various groups in that city advocated approval of the bond issue because Portland automobile owners wanted a good road to the sea. The state highway department became involved in planning the Columbia River highway and made a survey and estimates of cost for different sections.

The bond issue carried by 1,695 yes votes to 1,162 no votes. The yes vote was heavy at Clatskanie, Rainier, Goble and along the northwest section of the Columbia River highway. The no vote was emphatic in the south end of the county. Yankton voted 6 yes, 122 no; Vernonia 29 yes, 129 no; Warren 9 yes, 128 no; Mist 14 yes, 106 no; Houlton 15 yes, 102 no. The division in the county was deep and irreconcilable and political fallout was inescapable.

In May a grand jury completed a report critical of road plans, road expenditures, surveys, survey costs, the use of road funds, and procedures in making plans. It was a devasting report. It was signed by John G. Pringle of Vernonia, foreman, and G. W. Rodes, Will Karth of Yankton, Ben Van Cleave, J. F. Loyd, J. E. Johnson, and S. Saulser of Yankton.

By the end of July, 1914, petitions were being circulated to recall the county judge, two commissioners and the county attorney. The recall petitions were filed in late August, signed by 519 legal voters. A successful recall election was held on September 22, 2,800 votes being cast. The new slate won in what was a sectional battle. St. Helens, Scappoose, Warren supported the sitting officials; the inner county and the northern county voted to oust them.

The editor of the *St. Helens Mist* expressed his feelings: "Four honorable, upright, just and well-respected citizens have had their good names besmirched with slander and vilification . . . Whatever course the newly elected officers may pursue the fact will always remain that W. A. Harris, John Farr, Louis Flahrer and W.B. Dillard [the recalled four] are men of sterling worth and integrity."

The *Oregonian* in March, 1915, ran a story on the road situation in Columbia county. The misunderstanding, it said, was over finances. The county expected the state to help build the Columbia River highway as a state highway. The state engineer responsible for the various misunderstandings was forced to resign. The county spent $260,000 of its bonded money on the Columbia River highway, all north of Tide creek, and even so the road was not useable. Of the money which was to be spent on the St. Helens-Vernonia road, $50,000 was taken for the Columbia River highway. Cost overruns on every hand left the entire road picture in a state of chaos.

The editor of the *St. Helens Mist* was concerned for county harmony. The highway situation, he said, had divided localities against localities, neighbors against neighbors, friends against friends. And for what? "In the first place there never was any reason for it. There certainly has been no gain through it. Conditions today are no different . . . The present county court is exerting its most diligent effort to do what is right in the highway situation. This is nothing more than the former court was doing."

Another petition to recall the county judge and commissioners was started in January, 1916, by the taxpayers league. The court was spending too much money. It bought a five-passenger touring car for county use at an excessive price and it was used excessively.

The editor of the *St. Helens Mist* cautioned that the recall law was being abused. It was only a short time before recall movements were underway against both Rainier and Vernonia city officials.

On September 1, 1916, however, the editor of the *St. Helens Mist* put the matter which was troubling many people in perspective. Columbia county, he wrote, over the past four years had spent one million dollars on roads. "Can any sensible person think that we have gotten a million dollars worth of roads?" A million dollars for mostly dirt roads! "It is quite evident that we have not been getting nor are we now getting value for our dollars . . . The *Mist* says by all means build roads, but give the taxpayer something for the dollar he contributes."

Earlier, on March 3, 1916, the editor had looked at the Columbia River highway situation: "The opening of the Columbia River highway from Portland to Astoria on August 12, 1915, was a noteworthy event in that it marked the date when vehicular traffic for the first time traversed a highway down the valley of the Columbia River from Portland to the Pacific ocean. The event was commemorated by a large number of citizens in automobiles assembling at the Benson Hotel at 7 A.M. and going in a body, stopping at Clatskanie for lunch."

The two principal roads requiring attention were the Columbia River highway, demanded more by the residents of Multnomah county than by the Columbia county folk, and the St. Helens-Vernonia road, designated a county market road. George Wilson of Trenholm wrote a strongly worded letter to the *St. Helens Mist* in September, 1913, expressing what was the view of many in the interior. Good roads were needed to the interior farms of the county, the market roads, not automobile roads along the river for pleasure traffic. The argument for good roads for the farmer was illustrated by the fact that in the Scappoose area where roads were usable, produce was moved by auto freight at one-half the rate charged by the railroad.

Judson Weed of Vernonia said in October, 1920: ''I have waited for 45 years for a good road from Nehalem to St. Helens and when the Pittsburg-St. Helens road is completed and the farmers and residents of the Nehalem can come to the county seat without having to travel 50 unnecessary miles, it will be a cause of rejoicing with me.'' Judson Weed remembered hacking out the first wagon trail over Bunker Hill in 1879. When Washington Muckle began logging on Milton creek in 1874, the contact with the Scappoose plains was a mere trail along the slough and it took him a full day to get a load of freight as far up Milton creek as Herb Howard's place.

Political squabbling did not rock roads. And rocking roads cost money. The county road tax was raised from 3 mills in 1911 and 1912 to 9.5 mills in 1913, 7.55 mills in 1914, 8.9 mills in 1915.

Clatsop county, with fewer problems over inner county demands, had paved most of the Astoria-Seaside highway by 1916. The twenty miles could be driven in an hour. At that time a reporter drove from St. Helens to Seaside, 100 miles, in 6½ hours, clocking the various sections: St. Helens to Goble, good road, 12 miles in 45 minutes; from Goble, two miles of bad, rutted road needing chains in wet weather; four further miles to Rainier, good road; Rainier to Delena, eight miles, mostly good road, rocked; Delena to Clatskanie, 5½ miles, fair to rough, steep and narrow — sound horn! Mostly one track with few passing places; Clatskanie to Westport, fair road with loose rock, hard on tire. Naturally a driver expected a few tire blowouts on a trip. The road, he said, would be impassable in winter weather.

Thus, the county faced roads at a time when the hopeful were saying, "The automobile has long ceased to be a luxury to be enjoyed only by the very rich, and has become a business and commercial necessity. The passenger automobile has freed the farmer from isolation, has brought him miles nearer his buying and selling markets, and has saved him many working hours through the ground-covering ability of his automobile. The motor truck and farm tractor are increasing the amount of work he can accomplish at actually reduced expense."

The automobile was finding various uses. St. Helens in January, 1918, bought a fire truck for $1,400 equipped with chemical apparatus and fire hose. Steve Lampa, by 1921, was hauling logs into St. Helens on a log truck.

In March, 1917, Columbia county had 188 automobiles while the state had 34,000. Columbia county adopted a ten mill road tax to begin in 1918. A gasoline tax of one cent a gallon went into effect in March, 1919. M. O. Wilkins in the *Automobile Record* estimated that 100 automobiles were owned in St. Helens and the near vicinity. On June 4, 1917, Oregon voted a six million dollar bond issue for road development, part of it to go into developing the Columbia River highway. Simon Benson wrote a strong letter in favor of the levy. Every precinct in Columbia county voted in favor of the bond issue except Spitzenberg, Warren, Yankton.

Animosities and bickering over road issues ran deep. In May, 1916, a second recall election for members of the county court was held. Judge A. L. Clark was recalled, but commissioners A. E. Harvey and Judson Weed were not. The lopsided vote in the population centers indicated a sharp division. In no precinct in the county was the vote close. The editor of the *Rainier Review* proposed that the county be divided as it certainly was torn over road issues.

The market road from St. Helens to Pittsburg moved very slowly. It was admittedly in good shape as far as Trenholm. The ten miles from Trenholm to Pittsburg, especially over or around the Wilwerding hill, was the most serious problem area. With false starts and slow starts, little by little, a mile here and a mile there, contracts were let, work was partly done and roads reverted to impassability.

In July, 1919, the community of Vernonia invited the county to a picnic in an effort to show that the road ought to be completed. People were assured that the road was fairly good for a mountain road, but careful driving was necessary over the section west of Trenholm, especially over the Wilwerding hill. A caravan of autos left St. Helens at eight o'clock, in time to get to Vernonia for a one o'clock picnic. Some one hundred automobiles went over the road to Vernonia.

Four years and three months later the road was declared graded and rocked, an all-year road at last. In August, 1923, the editor of the *St. Helens Mist* in Glen Metsker's automobile made the thirty miles from St. Helens to Vernonia in an hour and a half, even though the road was rough in places. Judson Weed had to wait only forty-nine years for the road he wanted. Before the road was declared completed, the railroad made its way into Vernonia, this, too, after a long generation of anticipation.

The Portland, Astoria and Pacific Railroad Company built a track from Linnton to Vernonia, the first passenger train running on September 9, 1922. A St. Helens delegation joined in the celebration, 170 people going from the county seat via Linnton. The train arrived at Vernonia at 1 P.M., ahead of a special train from Portland with 200 passengers. The Nehalem valley, said one excited resident, "had waited 10,000 years for this!" A dinner and speaking in the park made a community celebration. Omar Spencer, born in Vernonia, was the climactic speaker at this important turning point in the life of the Nehalem valley. His father, Israel P. Spencer, died the November following, living just long enough to hear the long-awaited train whistle.

Regular once-a-day service ran from Portland to Keasey, twelve miles beyond Vernonia on Rock creek.

Columbia county first designated a speed cop in the sheriff's office in June, 1917. He was definitely not a traffic officer. He was, with the help of the county judge, out to get speeders — or to get fines! The speed limit was twenty-five miles an hour. During a ten day period in August, 1920, H. W. Weigle arrested twenty-one persons for speeding and Judge Hazen fined them. From August 8 to 31, forty-seven arrests yielded $823.70 in fines. The first ten days in September twenty-six persons were hauled before the judge for speeding. In December, Trig Forness, driver of the St. Helens-Portland auto stage, was arrested and charged with driving thirty-six miles an hour. He was fined $25 and put in jail for ten days. This was the first jail sentence in the county for speeding and was Trig Forness' fourth speeding offense. He apparently had to hurry to run his stage schedule which was then running three trips daily into Portland. During March, 1921, some sixty motorists paid $850 in fines.

Fines were profitable for the county. Judge Storia imposed $8,744.50 in fines involving speeding during 1923. Prohibition law violators also were prime targets and were fined $11,408.20 during the one year by Judge Storia.

The prohibition laws and man's taste for alcoholic beverages provided an equation making both problems and opportunities for the county. In November, 1914, Columbia county voted dry, 2,046 votes to 1,327. Only Goble, Prescott, Scappoose, and St. Helens Precinct No. 1 had small majorities for wet over dry. Clatskanie, in May, 1913, voted to go dry by forty-nine votes, effective January 1, 1914. Rainier, notorious for its saloon activities, had its saloons closed by vote of the city council in 1914.

One incident may illustrate what often happened in the county during the decade. Whether on some neighbor's tip or on general suspicion, two county officers set out to search the farm of John Wilwerding. His homestead at the crown of the hill west of Trenholm was well known. He had been a respected and prominent resident of the area for thirty years, serving as school board director and in other capacities.

The deputies testified in court that as they approached the house and announced themselves, Mrs. Wilwerding broke bottles which had contained liquid which smelled like liquor.

They followed a well-worn path to a cave in a hill and found a still in operation with mash and alcohol. They discovered John Wilwerding walking in the woods, and they found a barrel of homemade whiskey with a spigot in it behind a large stump.

Wilwerding was arrested but released on $500 bail. He was tried in August, 1922, before a jury of responsible citizens and found not guilty. He was apparently charged with possession, and possibly with manufacturing illegal liquor, although there was no tangible evidence of possession. The cave, still and barrel were not on his land, even though the worn path led from his door to the cave.

Wilwerding, raised in Luxembourg, was used to his daily drink of alcoholic beverage so his way of life did not fit well with the prohibition laws. But he was one of the many arrested who did not pay a fine to the county. He paid a good lawyer instead.

The sheriff's office was showing a profit from fines and fees. For 1921 the income exceeded $16,000, while the operating cost was $8,845. Fifty-five persons out of fifty-eight arrested were found guilty of prohibition violations and fined $9,830. Traffic offenders accounted for much of the other income.

XIII: COLUMBIA COUNTY:
CHANGING, YET UNCHANGED

*I have instituted inquiries to correct tricks of memory,
and striven against temptations to exaggerate, in order
to preserve . . . a fairly true record of a vanishing life
period.*

Thomas Hardy, 1912

In the spring of 1914 Columbia county had 131 students
graduating from the eighth grade. The fifty-four school
districts had only four high schools. What to do about
schools in the sparsely settled areas of the county was
becoming an increasingly urgent question. The Nehalem
valley had 200 school pupils scattered in fifteen schools with
seventeen teachers. The sixteen pupils seeking high school
work found no adequate high school within reach.

In August, 1914, a public meeting was held in Houlton
with representatives from seven adjacent school districts to
consider the matter of a union high school district. Uther
Clark was named chairman of the meeting and Iris Oliver
secretary, both from the newly formed Columbia Heights
school district which had split off from the Houlton district.
A writer in the *St. Helens Mist* commented, "A beautiful
view of the grand old Columbia River . . . with several snow-
capped mountain peaks. The lights of Portland are plainly
visible at night . . . during the day a wonderfully beautiful
landscape . . . The road along this place is well improved and
macadam . . . Truly a beautiful place and deserving the
name Columbia Heights."

The school districts up the Milton creek valley had some
responsive leadership. W. H. Dolman had earlier remarked

on the uniqueness of a community where a school, church and public hall arrived before a hotel, saloon and blacksmith shop. The Milton creek valley had several schools, churches, public halls and no saloon west of Houlton until one reached Nehalem valley.

The school at Trenholm, District No. 43, "is in the lead of all our rural schools," reported the county school superintendent, J. W. Allen, "and is still making improvements such as beautification of the school grounds, permanent walks, and electric lights. It is the only rural school in the county that has electric lights." The Yankton school was serving hot lunches in December, 1915.

No formal action came from the Houlton meeting, but the fact of the meeting indicated a concern. Vernonia in 1915 consolidated school districts 14, 27, 47, 51 and 55 into a union high school district, thus joining St. Helens, Scappoose, Rainier and Clatskanie in having four-year high schools.

In the fall of 1918 Rainier bused twelve high school pupils from Goble, Beaver Home and Prescott.

St. Helens had problems in getting the idea of a union high school district considered. The 1914 meeting failed to develop any program. St. Helens agreed to accept high school students from other districts on a tuition basis, the home district of the pupil paying the $125 tuition. Thus, pupils came from Warren, Deer Island, Bachelor Flat, Columbia Heights, Yankton, Houlton. How pupils got to school seemed to be a question of constant concern and disagreement. The Yankton school directors, thinking that some of their young pupils were walking too far in winter weather, in December, 1917, agreed to pay the board for three young pupils who were boarded with Mrs. Steve Lampa, near the school house.

Ira Howard walked from Yankton to St. Helens to high school in 1919, as other students must have also. St. Helens had tried busing high school students from outlying districts in 1920-1921, but transporting six or seven pupils in to school had cost $20 a month and the school board abandoned the plan as not worth the expense. In 1922 the Yankton school district voted 22 for and 20 against paying one-half the cost of transporting the students to St. Helens high school provided the St. Helens district would pay the other half. The contract was let with the district paying W. Johnson $75 a month to transport the twelve pupils.

The St. Helens school building burned just after the opening of the school in September, 1918. The community engaged in discussion over what kind of building or buildings should replace it, and where to build. In December the district voted bonds to build a new John Gumm school to house both the grade school and the high school on the former site at a projected cost of $37,000. The vote was 54 yes, 27 no. The building was ready to open for the fall term, 1919.

During the 1924-1925 school year the proposal for a union high school in St. Helens was discussed with more than the usual acrimony. The principal issue was the projected location of the proposed new high school. Vocal residents of outlying districts protested that all St. Helens wanted was for them to help pay for a new high school building. The vote on unification was held March 14, 1925. St. Helens, of course, wanted the union high school district and voted 645 to 15 in favor. Two small districts remote from St. Helens also favored unification: Canaan 26 to 1 and Trenholm 20 to 1. Five other districts, all closer to St. Helens, voted adversely. None of them had their own high schools. Opponents had objected to the projected school being built in or near downtown St. Helens. Others with sheer economic motives objected to helping pay for a new high school building. But personality clashes and suspicion also played a large part in the campaigning and the vote.

Deer Island and Columbia City had extremists who shouted against being pushed around by a big neighbor. Remnants of the road squabbling carried over. Deer Island voted 91 to 10 against union; Columbia City was 89 to 11 against. Bachelor Flat was 44 to 15 against, Yankton 58 to 23 against, Columbia Heights 15 to 13 against — the only district with a balanced vote. The total vote was 743 for union, 377 against; yet the proposal lost, for five districts vetoed the idea. Tommie Holstein bought a 35-passenger bus to transport the high school students from Trenholm and Yankton to St. Helens.

St. Helens went ahead on its own to build a new high school on the proposed site. It had years to wait before a union district was formed.

St. Helens had sixty-five students in the high school in September, 1916, seventy-six high school pupils in September, 1918, and 94 in September, 1919. It graduated twelve seniors in 1920, including the author, and fourteen in 1921. Clatskanie had forty-three students attending high school in September, 1918, graduating six in May, 1920. Vernonia had twenty-six high school students in 1922, graduating six in May.

In 1916 the county had about one hundred women teaching, averaging $60 a month in salary, and nineteen men averaging $100 a month. Some were high school teachers, who averaged $13.50 a month more than grade school teachers. High school principals averaged $145; grade school principals $90.

In February, 1920, J. W. Allen, the county school superintendent, reported, "The schools of the county are in excellent condition and good work is being accomplished."

The editor of the *St. Helens Mist* ended the year 1922 with a hopeful look toward the future: "The four sawmills are running steadily, two of them double time. There are few unemployed men." Although the school superintendent might have thought conditions good, and the editor might have been hopeful, the school board knew that voters resisted taxes. The board abandoned its rudimentary busing program because it cost $20 a month, and in March reduced teachers' salaries for the next year. Seventy-five percent of all Columbia county teachers were first year teachers.

The question of what would pay best on Columbia county farms seemed to come up frequently. In 1915 Yankton farmers expressed divergent opinions. Ray Tarbell said, "poultry." Lawrence and Guy Tarbell said, "cattle — with potatoes as a sideline." Robert Jeffries wanted a more

The 1920 St. Helens High School graduating class. Left to right, front row: Elsie Morley, Mabel Davies, Ethel Smith, Florence Van Gilder, Louise Anderson, Ruby Ward; back row, Max Wilson, author Egbert Oliver, Oury Hisey, Eduard Richardsen, Martin Briggs (who died before graduating), William Dodd. The class stands on the south steps of the John Gumm school.

diversified line, with gardening, small fruits and potatoes. Over the county orchards were being reduced while cattle herds and grain acreage increased. Marketing farm produce was still a problem.

Louis Rosasco, an Italian truck gardener who came to the St. Helens area from New York in 1905, led a movement to organize a stock-company cannery for the St. Helens area in the fall of 1914. He invited participation in financing the cannery and asked farmers to plant produce for it. String beans were to be the principal crop.

In July the Columbia River Canning and Produce Company elected officers: president, Lawrence Tarbell; treasurer, William Phillips; secretary, Charles D. White; general manager, Louis Rosasco. By August the farmers were bringing in crops and the cannery was turning out cans of beans. It had a capacity of 8,000 cans a day, but rarely reached that amount. The author, as a thirteen-year-old, washed those cans and sent them down the line to be filled for seven and one-half cents an hour.

The A. W. Berry and Company Cannery in Rainier was canning salmon, smelt and caviar according to an 1883 article on Columbia county; however, the county farmers had to wait a long time for the canning market for their produce.

Rosasco wanted the cannery to handle a general run of fruit, berries and vegetables, but the volume and equipment hardly supported such general canning activities. The cannery continued to handle mainly string beans and cabbage made into sauerkraut. It paid farmers $20,000 in 1916, with $8,000 going to the cannery work force.

In August, 1917, Emma Tarbell wrote that they had 1,300 pounds of beans on their first picking. The pole beans had six or eight pickings. "We had over $200 worth of beans last year on an acre." Bert Tarbell succeeded Lawrence Tarbell as the president of the cannery association. In the spring of 1920 Alice Brown wrote, "Frank has a meeting of his cannery association to attend. We hope the company will do well this season . . . we hope there may be dividend, this year, though expenses are pretty heavy the first two years."

The cannery was paying the farmers $40 a ton in 1917. In September the bean cannery had sixty women and girls working and needed forty more. Farmers were paid for their crops and a few workers received wages, but it did not pay dividends. Louis Rosasco moved with his family to Los Gatos, California in 1922 and the cannery boom ended in St. Helens.

Clatskanie, in October, 1918, had a plant canning cabbage, with 1,700 tons contracted.

The Allen and Hendricks Packing Company of Rainier in 1925 was projecting fifty acres of beets for canning. The company wanted to can fish, fruit, and vegetables and was contracting farmers. In the spring of 1926 it opened a branch in St. Helens. This Rainier company had paid out to growers and cannery labor in 1925 $73,986.98. Around 60,000 cases of string beans, various amount of strawberries, blackberries, raspberries, loganberries, Royal Anne cherries and dark red Detroit beets were processed. Its vegetable pack had doubled in four years. Money payment to county growers and laborers doubled in one year to $153,026.14 for 1926. But the cannery situation was unsettled. The Rainier plant did not process fruit in 1928; a cannery in Longview would take the fruit, but that involved river shipment.

St. Helens wanted a cannery. Strawberries were barreled there and sent to Seattle for processing into jam. Various farmers had tried growing strawberries as a cash crop over the years, but the assessor's office in 1920 showed only twenty-eight acres of strawberries in the county. Yankton accounted for most of those acres because various farmers had met there in 1919 and agreed to plant strawberries.

The Brinn farm had a crew of strawberry pickers in the field in June, 1922, shipping a ton from the first picking. Brinns shipped 1,500 crates on the train to Portland, getting $1.65 a crate. They had eight acres of strawberries, setting out four more acres in October, 1923. By 1927 Brinn had twenty-five acres of strawberries, ten acres of raspberries. He later sold his 166 acre farm to C. W. Phillips for about $20,000.

The St. Helens Creamery Association was organized in August, 1915. It did much better than the cannery association, both in serving the farmers and the stockholders. It was from the first a successful project. A. H. Tarbell of Warren was president, P. C. Jacobsen, secretary. Directors were Than Brown, F. H. Adams, and K. F. Larson. In its second year the creamery produced a hundred thousand pounds of butter and paid out to farmers forty thousand dollars.

Dairying continued over the first quarter of the century to produce about forty per cent of the agricultural output of the county. The number of cattle and the butter and milk yield grew in about the same ratio as the county grew and developed. The 5,755 cattle of 1890 (twenty per cent milk cows) reported in the census became 7,802 cattle (4,515 dairy cows) in the 1910 census. In 1930 twenty-eight per cent of the county was in 1,667 farms, mostly owner-operated. The census showed 13,343 cattle.

The dairy and breeding farms near Scappoose continued to be impressive in their production. The Yankton area received attention for its animal and poultry farming. Herb Howard increased his Hereford stock and Than Brown took prizes for his Chester White hogs. Ray Tarbell's poultry was outstanding.

D. C. Howard, the Columbia county agricultural agent in 1919 wrote, "Yankton, long famous for its progressive farmers, good farm products, and high class Shorthorn cattle will henceforth also be known as the leading Jersey center of Columbia county." The point of this extreme statement was that Fred Briggs and Than Brown had bought several daughters of the champion bull Golden Glow's Chief. Cattlemen from Yankton attending the Pacific International Livestock Exposition included Fred Briggs, Lawrence Tarbell, Guy Tarbell, Ray Tarbell, Than Brown, Joe Sobieski, A. Markkanen, Cal Howard, Jim Van Tassel, Frank Rice, Leland Rice, Steve Lampa, J. N. Brinn.

The Yankton farmers were investing in registered cattle: the Tarbells, $1,000 for a Shorthorn heifer; A. A. Markkanen, $1,500 for a Jersey cow; Than Brown, $550 for a

Jersey cow. John Farr of Warren paid $500 for a Holstein cow. Delena farmers also were developing herds of Jersey cattle.

One of the important agricultural developments of the county in the early twenties was the diking of the bottom land along Scappoose bay, the reclaiming from lowland flooding of over six thousand acres. This became valuable and productive farm land.

About that time Scappoose voted to incorporate as a city, the population then about 400. It had, on March 25, 1917, dedicated the Congregational church building, "one of the most substantial church edifices in the county." The Rev. L. R. Dyott, minister of the First Congregational church of Portland, had delivered the dedication sermon. Pastor at Scappoose was the Rev. C. H. Johnson.

The Warren grange took a spurt and doubled its membership in 1919, becoming the leading grange chapter in the state. But Warren received a blow to its pride when the railroad closed the station and removed its agent, leaving Warren a mere flag stop. The apparent reason was the falling off of freight and passenger traffic as highway use increased.

The St. Helens Flour Milling Company began business in 1918 and continued operation successfully over the decade of the twenties.

Tom Johnson, a wealthy Portland black, ran a hog ranch up Milton creek from Yankton, hauling garbage from the city for feed. His hog ranch was run by a local foreman and a couple of hired hands. It broke into the news when the hired hands killed the foreman and fled the state. The two were apprehended — one in Tennessee, one in Idaho — and returned for trial and sentencing for murder.

E. H. Seeman of Goble made farm news of a more promising nature. He planted an acre and a half of ginseng, thus having the largest planting on the Pacific Coast. This exotic plant for use in Chinese medical practice was reported to be very profitable if it could be successfully grown. E. G.

Malcolm of St. Helens and Mr. Bodin of Mayger also planted ginseng.

Joe Koller, back of Deer Island, also tried something different. He had a herd of ninety goats and made Swiss cheese for the Portland market.

In September, 1915, the St. Helens Women's Club organized a loaning library to be staffed by volunteers. It was open a couple of hours a week with thirty-five books, some given to the library, but mostly sent on a loan basis from the state library. The first book purchase, and that not for some time, was the American Winston Churchill's *Inside the Cup*. In 1918 the library purchased Churchill's *The Dwelling Place of Light* and the year's best seller, H. G. Well's *Mr. Britling Sees It Through*. By that time the library had 300 volumes of its own, plus those borrowed from the state library.

The Deer Island Women's Club followed suit and opened a lending library, largely using state library books, in June, 1920.

Alice Brown of Yankton borrowed books directly from the state library by mail instead of using the St. Helens library. She had been a school teacher in her girlhood in Maine and thought of herself as a woman much interested in education and personal development. She and her family may not have been unrepresentative of the reading practices in Columbia county, partial to Joseph C. Lincoln, B. M. Bower and James Whitcomb Riley. Alice Brown wrote to her sister-in-law Anna Tarbell: "Do you take any time to read? This summer I have read Henry Van Dyke's *Little Rivers*, a charming book, and *The Hidden Garden* by Frances Hodgon Burnett . . . Oh, if you have not *all* of Gene Stratton-Porter's books . . . especially *Freckles* and *Michael O'Halloran*. I love *The Harvester* best of all."

The movies came to take care of the county's entertainment need. St. Helens had at first scant offerings, but by 1916, when the public library boasted of having two hundred books, only fifty of which were on loan from the state library, the Strand Movie Palace was showing pictures almost every day. Charlie Chaplin, Francis X. Bushman, and even Pearl White were billed — and Bret Harte, with his dead-eye look and his quick gun, was soon to follow. *The Birth of the Nation*, hooded KKK's and all, received considerable advertising. Dustin Farnum in Booth Tarkington's *The Gentleman from Indiana*, Marguerite Clark in Mark Twain's *The Prince and the Pauper*, and even Thomas Hardy's *Tess of the D'Urbervilles* made their appearance. Admission was five and fifteen cents. Mary Pickford was popular in 1916.

Mr. and Mrs. Charles Wickstrom of Scappoose enjoyed a new Victrola in December, 1918. The Clatskanie Methodist church installed a bathroom in the parsonage. The Plymouth Congregational church at St. Helens organized the Orpheus Club with nine voices and gave much-appreciated concerts. The Rev. A. R. Spearow, a very accomplished man, was the organizer and director. He also held the pole vaulting record in the state and on the Pacific Coast.

Sabastian F. "Heine" Heumann, who married Miss Hilma Morton, owned and operated the Houlton bakery. He was, in 1920, well and favorably known in St. Helens. Orphaned at age two in Germany, apprenticed to a baker at age eleven, he came to the Houlton bakery at the beginning of the anti-German sentiment during World War I and found himself the object of much abuse. By sheer personal effort and magnetism he overcame that animosity and became a universal favorite. Heine became a St. Helens school director and was, for half a century, an able civic leader.

In 1923 radios were in the news and were advertised for fifty dollars and up. It was expected that an audience of a million people would hear a national hookup broadcast of the singing of "Home, Sweet Home" on its centennial. Louis F. Barger had the first radio in Yankton, in January, 1924, and invited friends in to enjoy "excellent music and interesting programs that come from distant places and which the radio snatches from the air."

President Calvin Coolidge's Washington Day address was broadcast by linking thirty-eight stations over the nation, including KGW of Portland. John L. Storla installed his private radio receiving set in the John Gumm school so that the students might hear the president speak.

A golf club was organized in St. Helens and a golf course was developed where Herb Howard had logged thirty-five years before. A J.C. Penney store and a Piggly Wiggly grocery store came to St. Helens. A Kiwanis club chapter was organized in February, 1927.

The three daughters of Joe and Jennie Sobieski — Agnes, Grace, and Hattie — all graduated from Monmouth Normal School in 1927. Their grandfather, Frank Sobieski, age 85, died in April, 1927. He had settled in the Polish community west of Trenholm in the early 1890s and was buried in the Yankton Hillcrest cemetery.

Charles W. Emerson, father of the large Emerson family of early settlers, was hit by a train at the Houlton crossing and died soon after the accident in late January, 1924. He was an old man and, apparently unaware of the train, walked into the side of the engine and was hit by the drive shaft.

An article on Columbia county published in Portland in 1883 said, "comparatively little farming is done . . . the lumbering business absorbing the attention of the people." Some people had thought farming, promoted farming, boosted and planned farming in the county for forty years and still timber was king. Apples and fruit, dairying, potatoes, hay and grain — each had had its boosters and adherents; but the timber kept on growing. A logging railroad, built into the Nehalem during the war years, by March, 1918, was hauling out of the valley a million feet of logs a day. Seven camps and a thousand men were attacking the forests. A city appropriately named Neverstil was started.

"The principal industry in Columbia county is lumbering," ran an editorial in the *St. Helens Mist*. A drive over the St. Helens-Pittsburg road in the 1980s shows twice as much timber land as farm land. The once thriving settlements at Peris, Valley, Trenholm are gone and only an occasional country home breaks the almost continuous stands of timber.

A sawmill first appeared in the county in 1849. Mills were still dominant during the twenties. St. Helens in 1928 could boast of having the largest wage per capita of any city in the United States. The varied McCormick interests gave variety to the milling operations — sawmill, shipyard, creosote plant, broom handle factory and others. Up and down the county the plant whistle was the heartbeat of the people.

Life in the county changed, but timber remained. The quarries of the county were supplying paving blocks to Portland in 1883 and for a decade into the twentieth century the rock of the county looked like a promising industry. With the coming of concrete highways the paving block specialists were out of work.

As the nineteenth century ended, six steamers ran regular schedules on the river. The steamer *America* made its last scheduled run in 1929, the last boat to serve the county on a scheduled basis. The railroad came, and trains went up and down the county half a dozen times a day; but with the advent of the automobile and better roads, passenger trains grew fewer and fewer, then finally disappeared.

Charles H. Briggs opened his Yankton store in 1896. When he died in 1916, his son Fred had already long been operating the business, a thriving community institution. Fred Briggs sold the store in 1922 to Tommie Holstine (whose family name had been changed from Holstein), who sold it to G. A. Bowen. Bowen moved the store from its longtime location in 1927 to the Redman hall. The hall, which had been the lodge and festive dance center for the community, witnessed the gradual death of this country store. Roads and automobiles ended the life of many a rural country store as Piggly Wiggly and J. C. Penney came to town.

The life of Columbia county, however, went on with continuing changes but no major disruptions as the pioneers dropped off one by one.